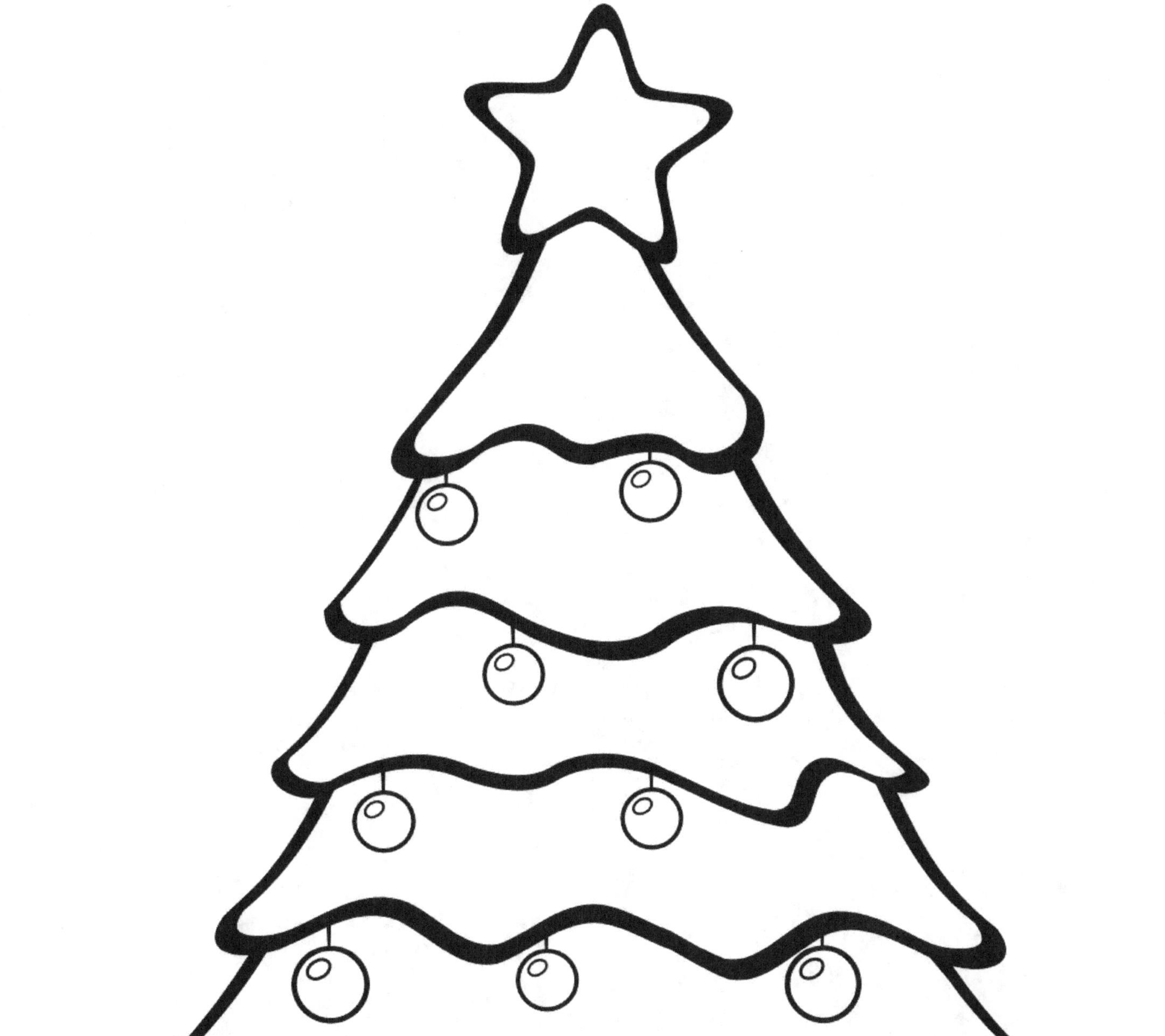

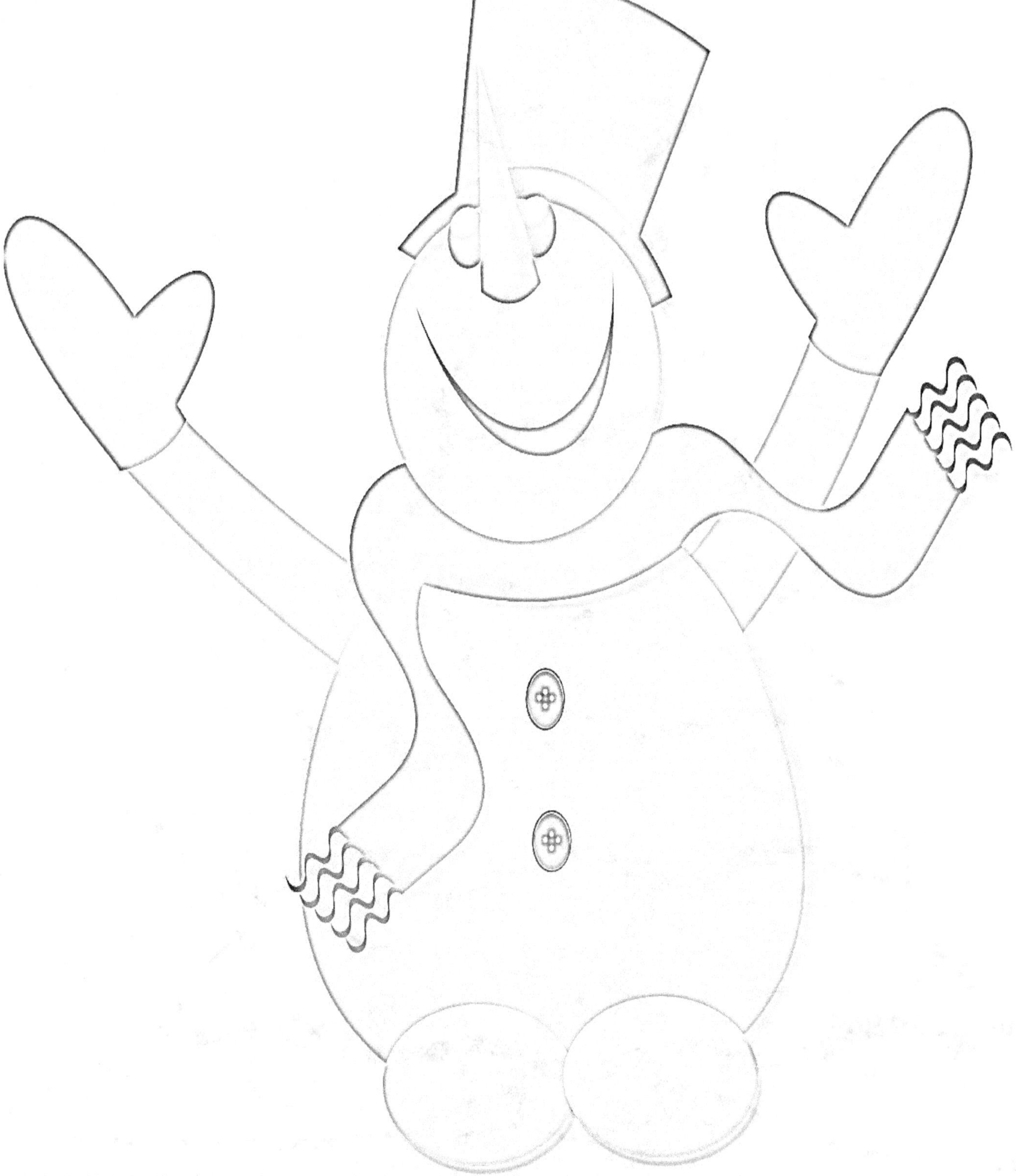

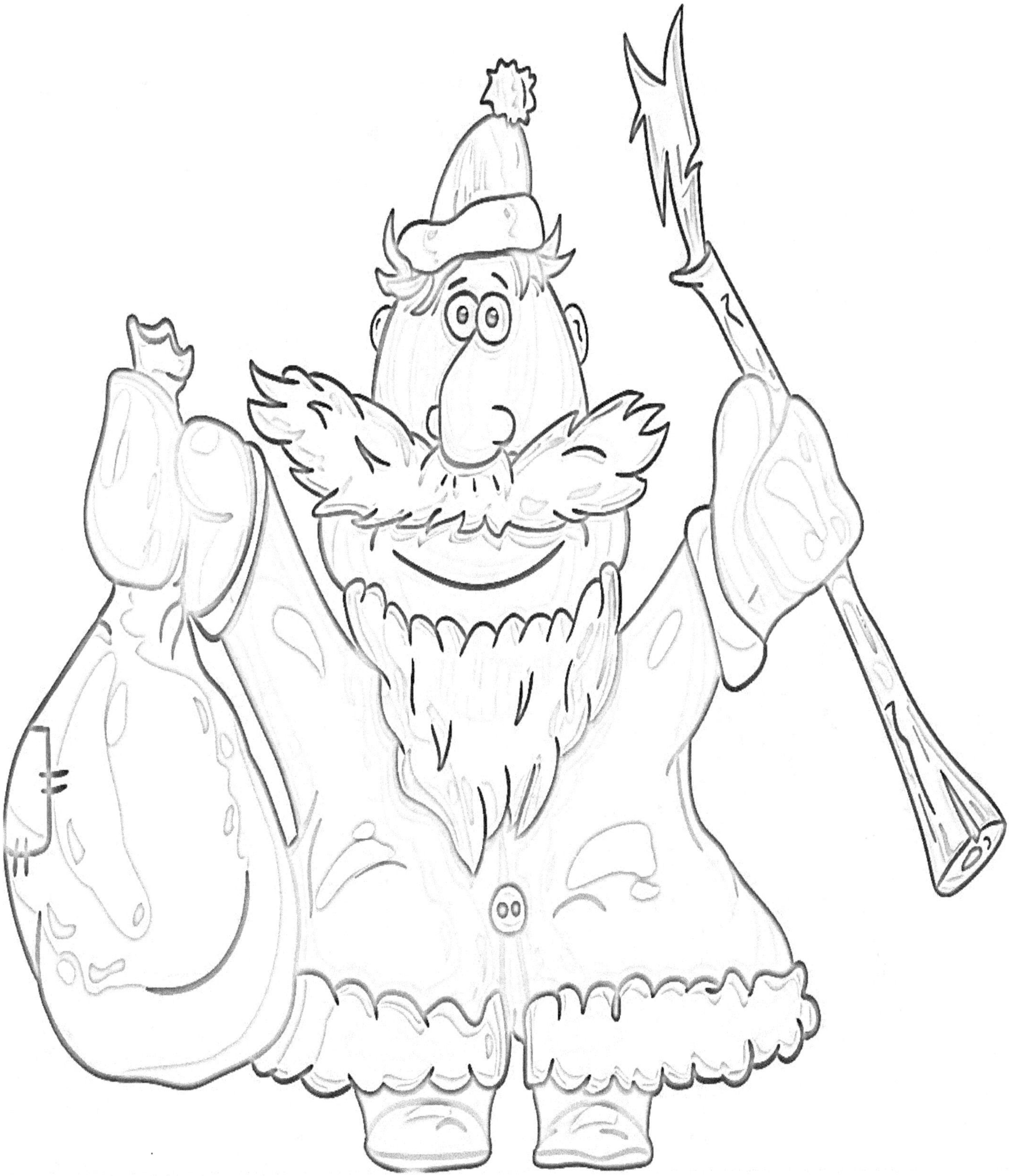

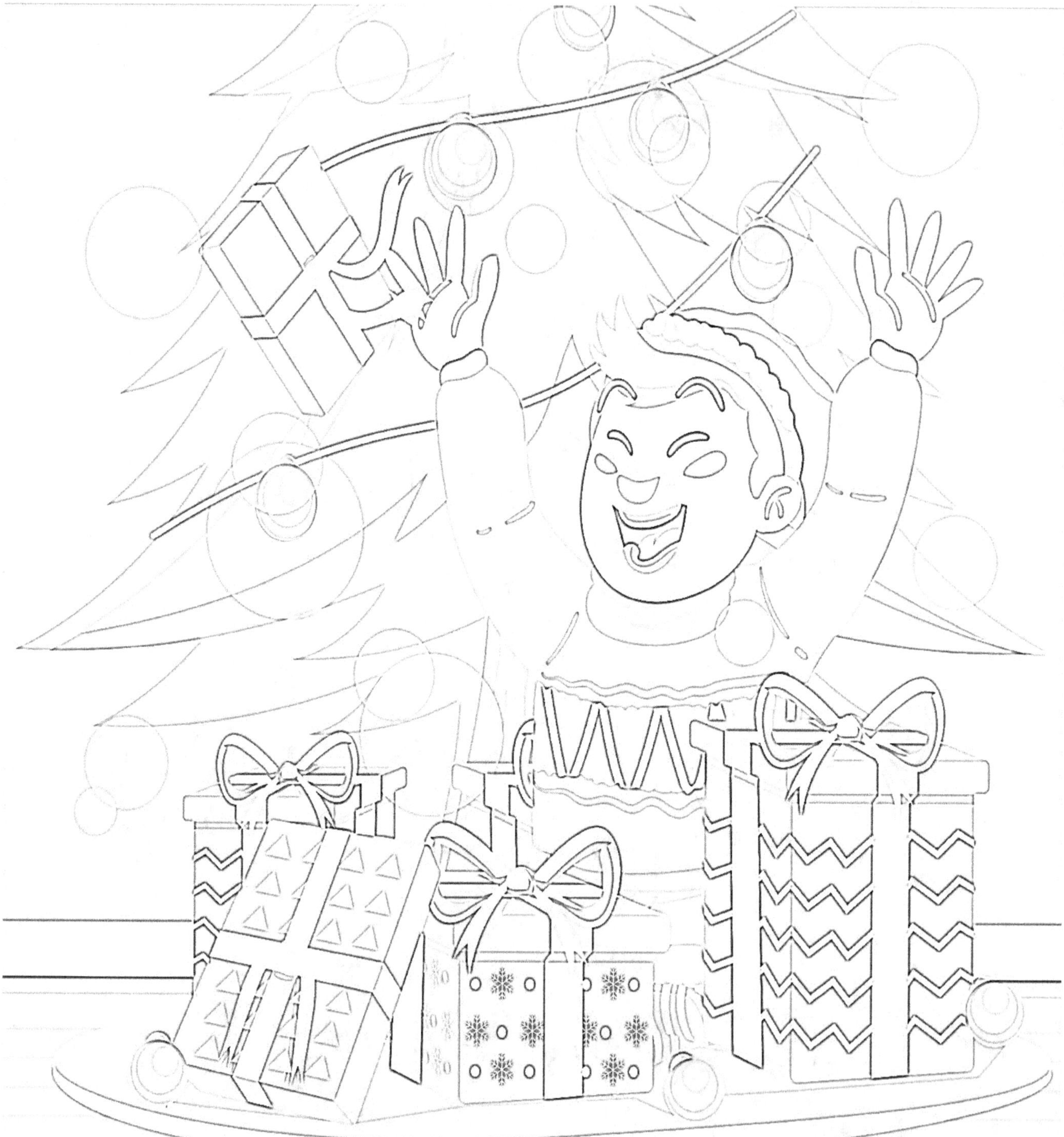

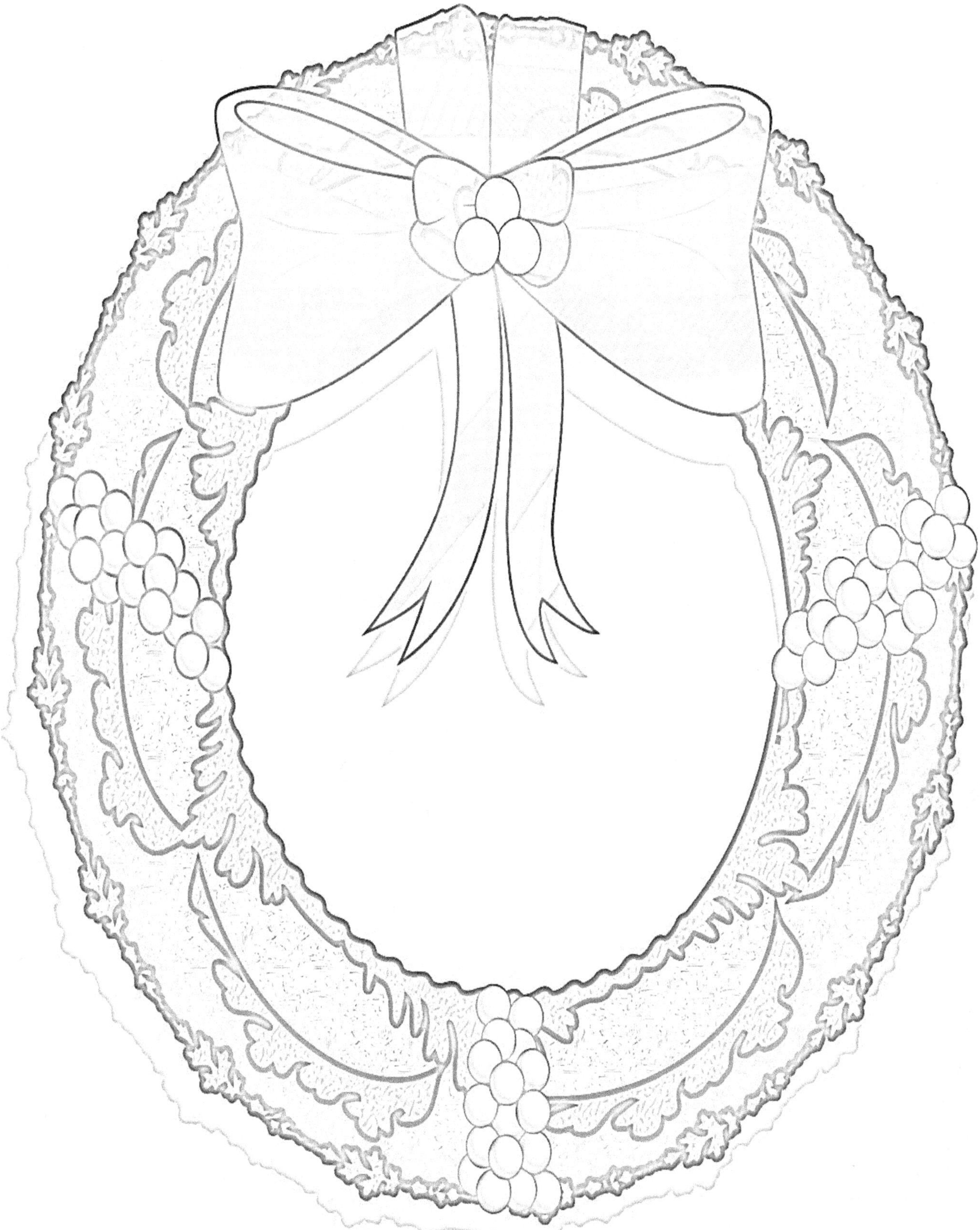

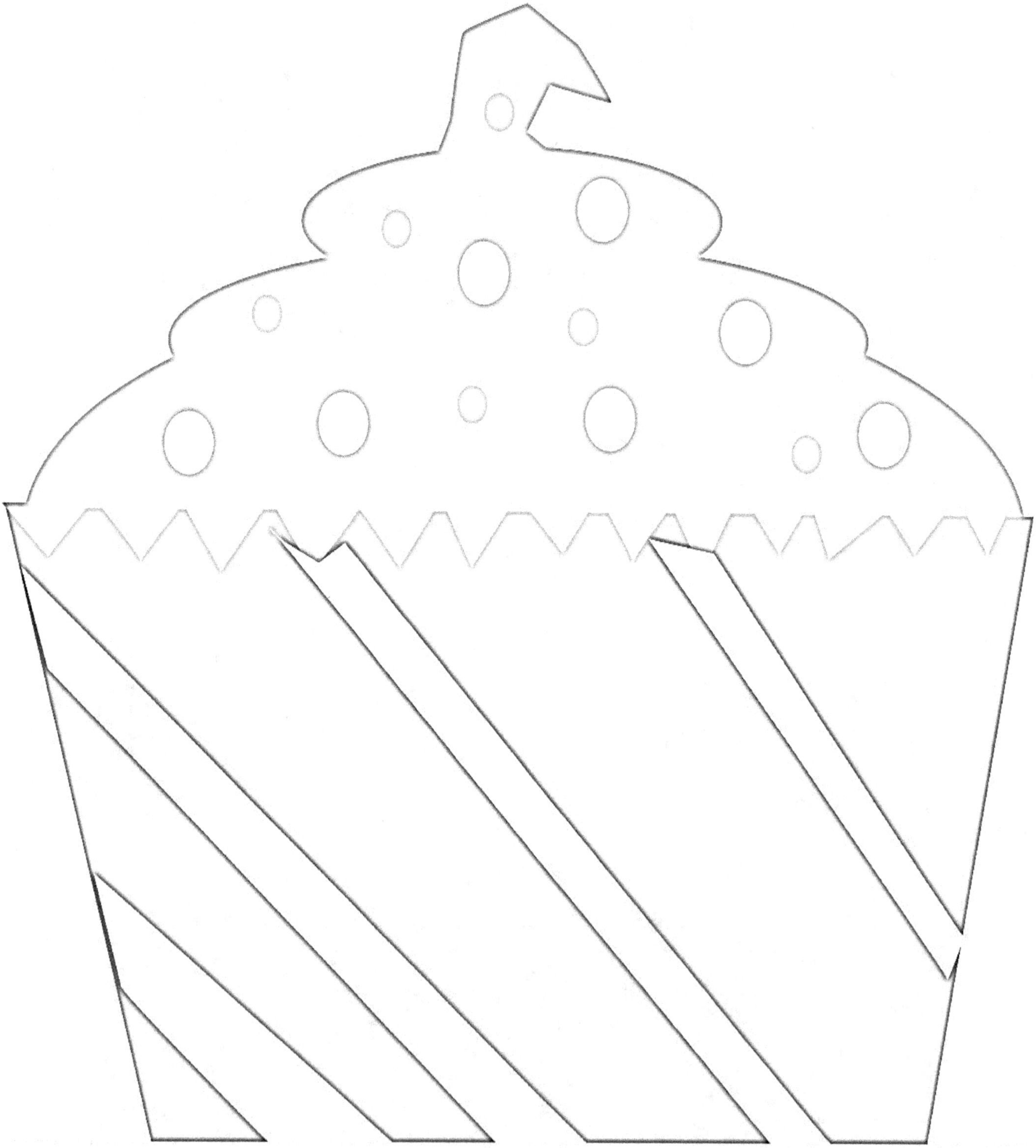

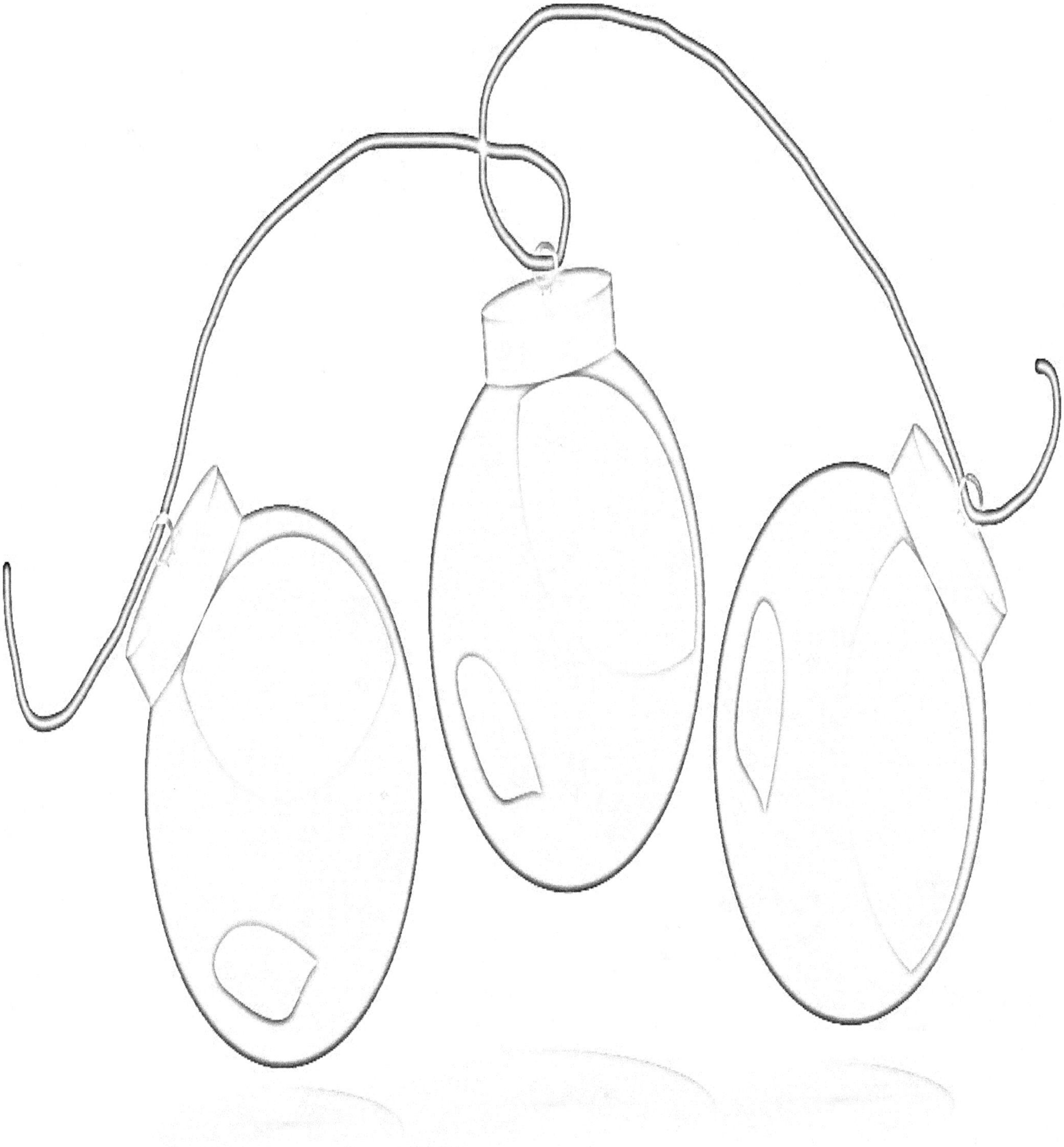

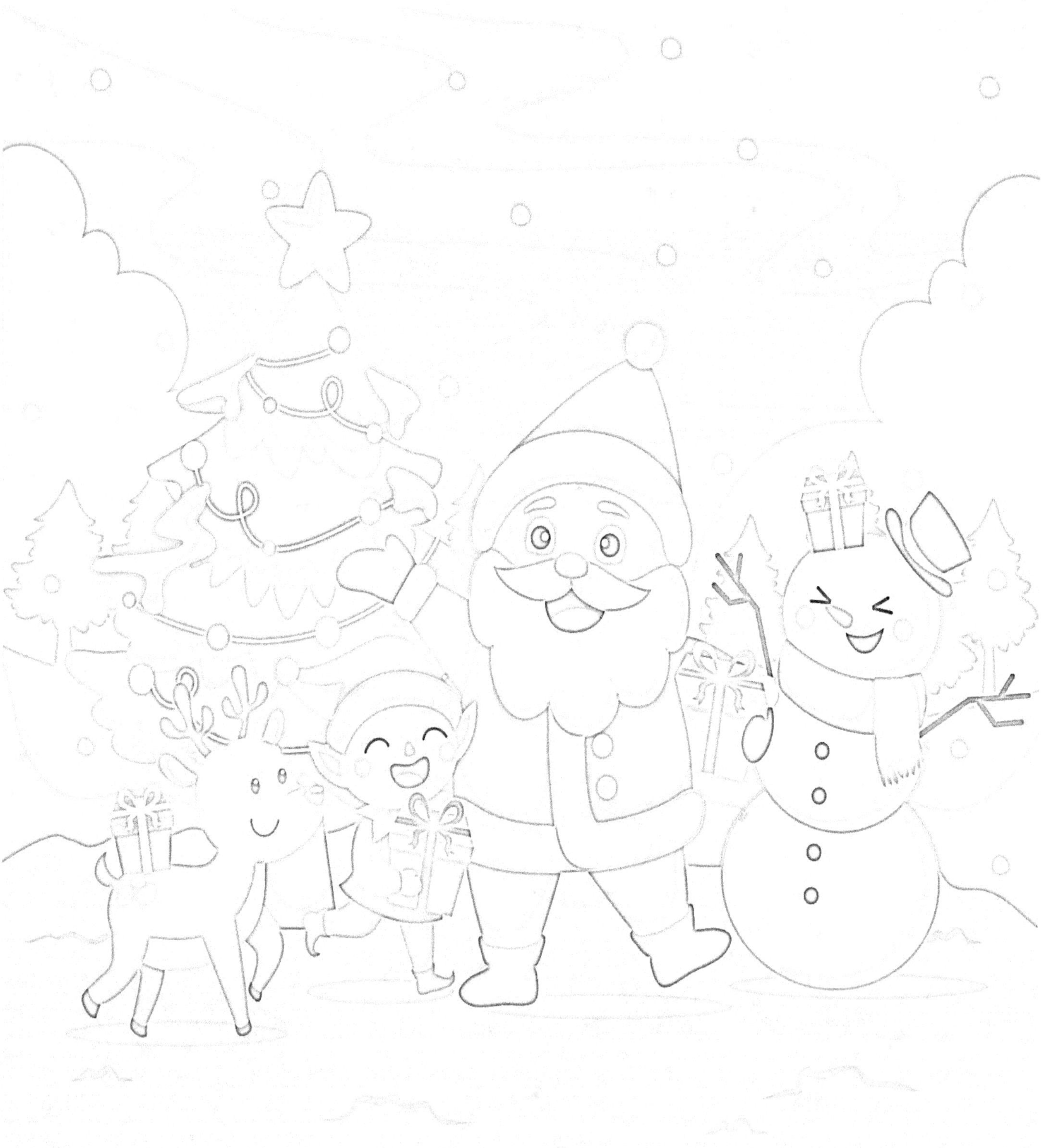

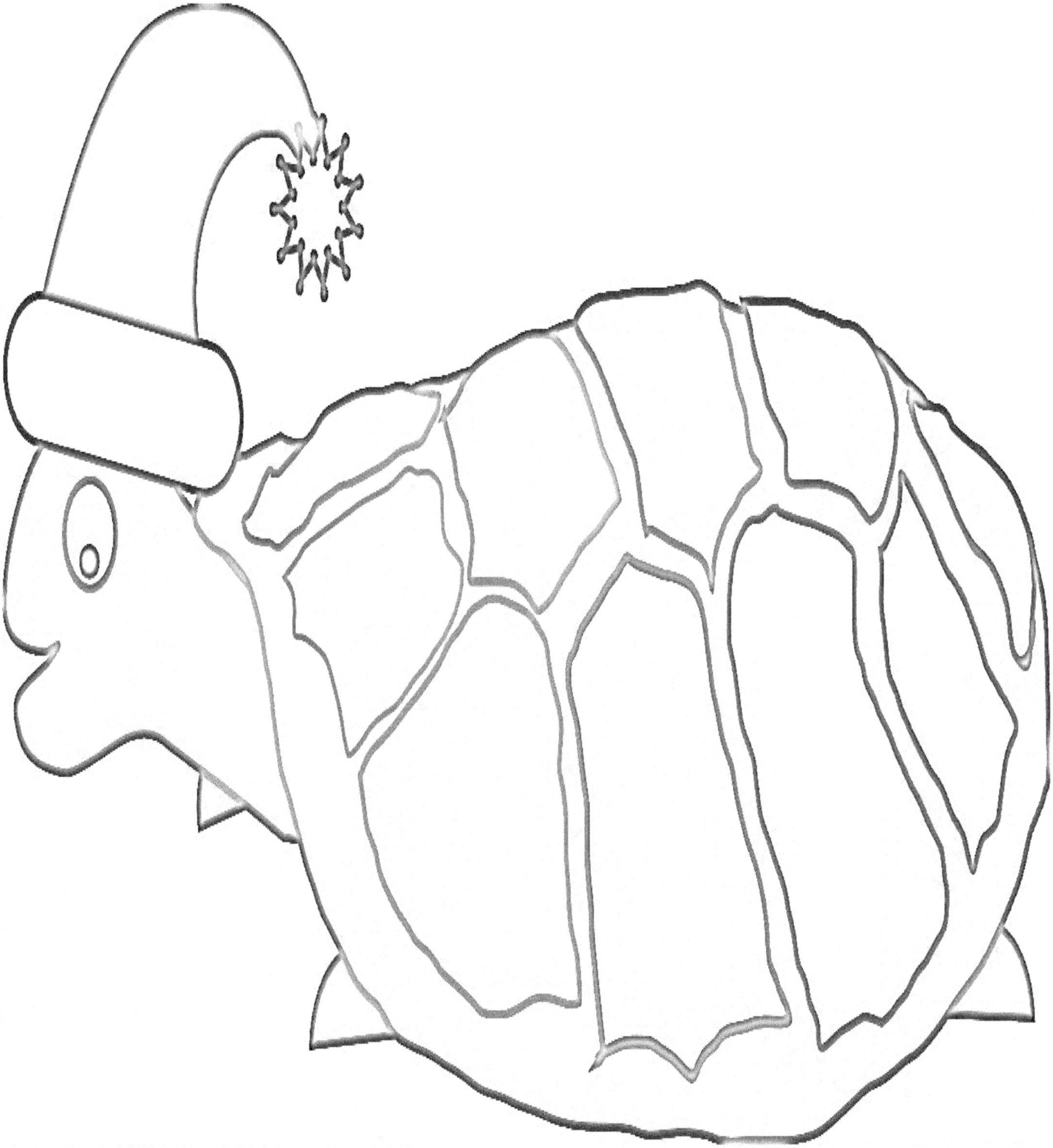

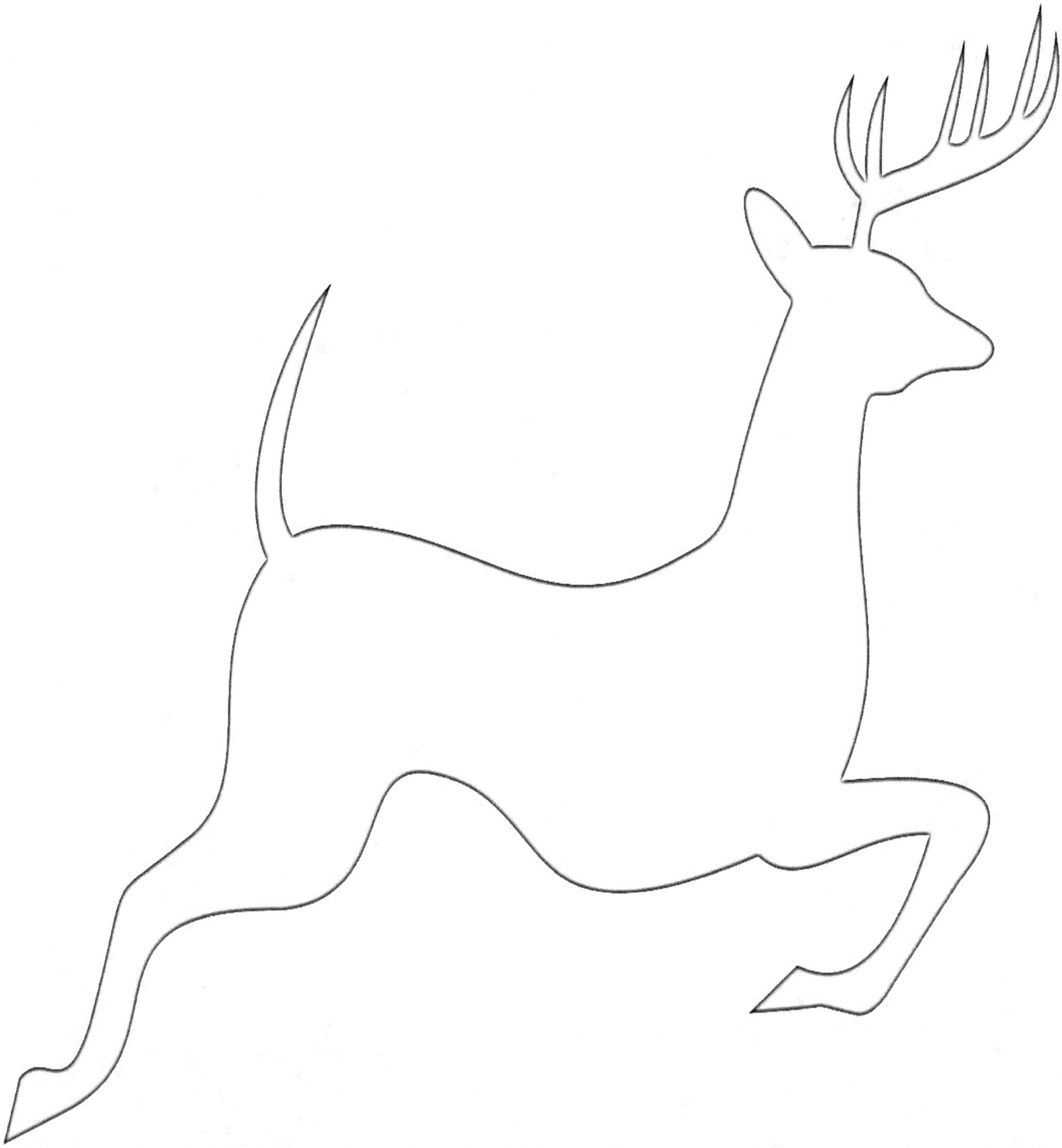

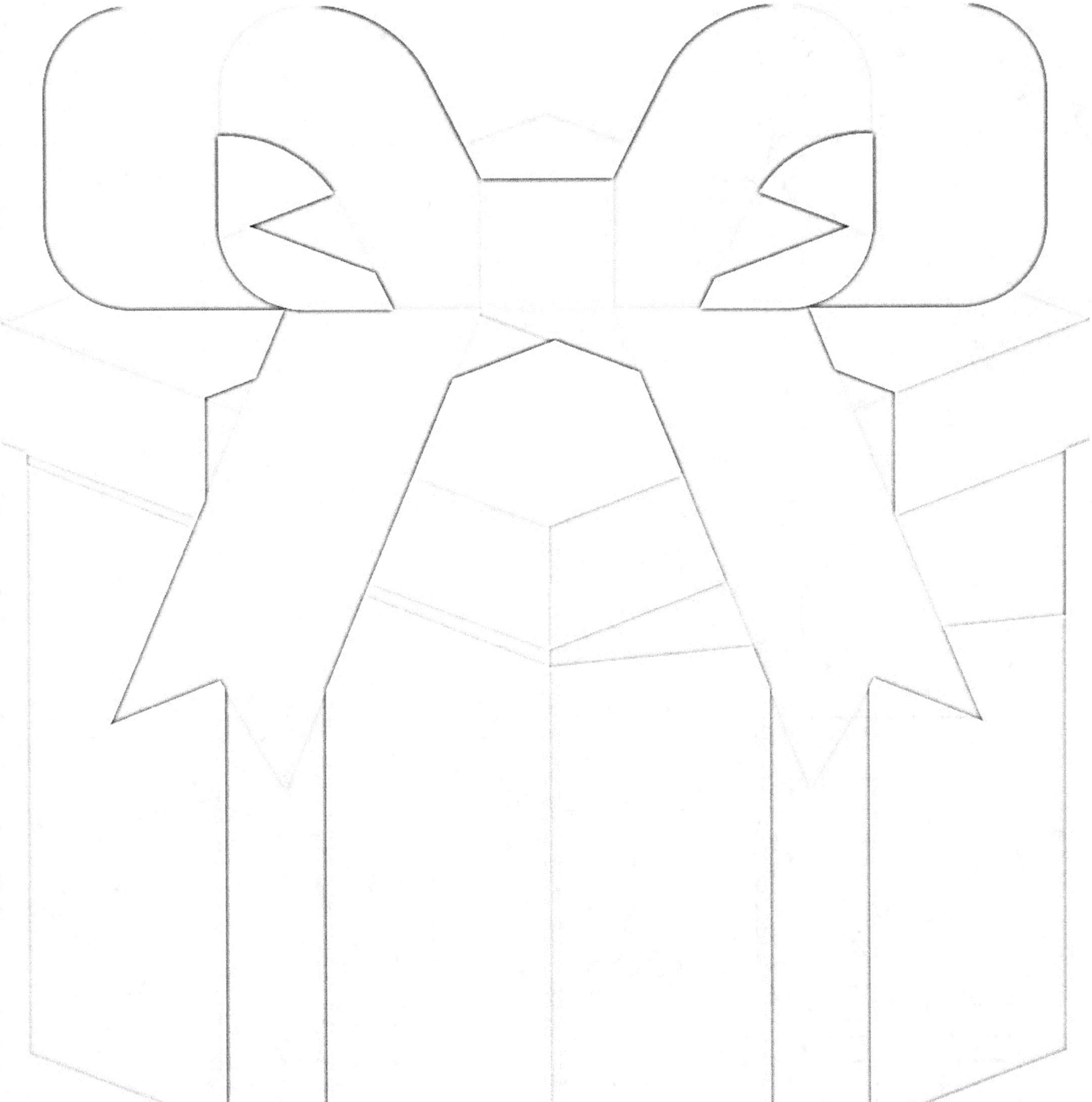

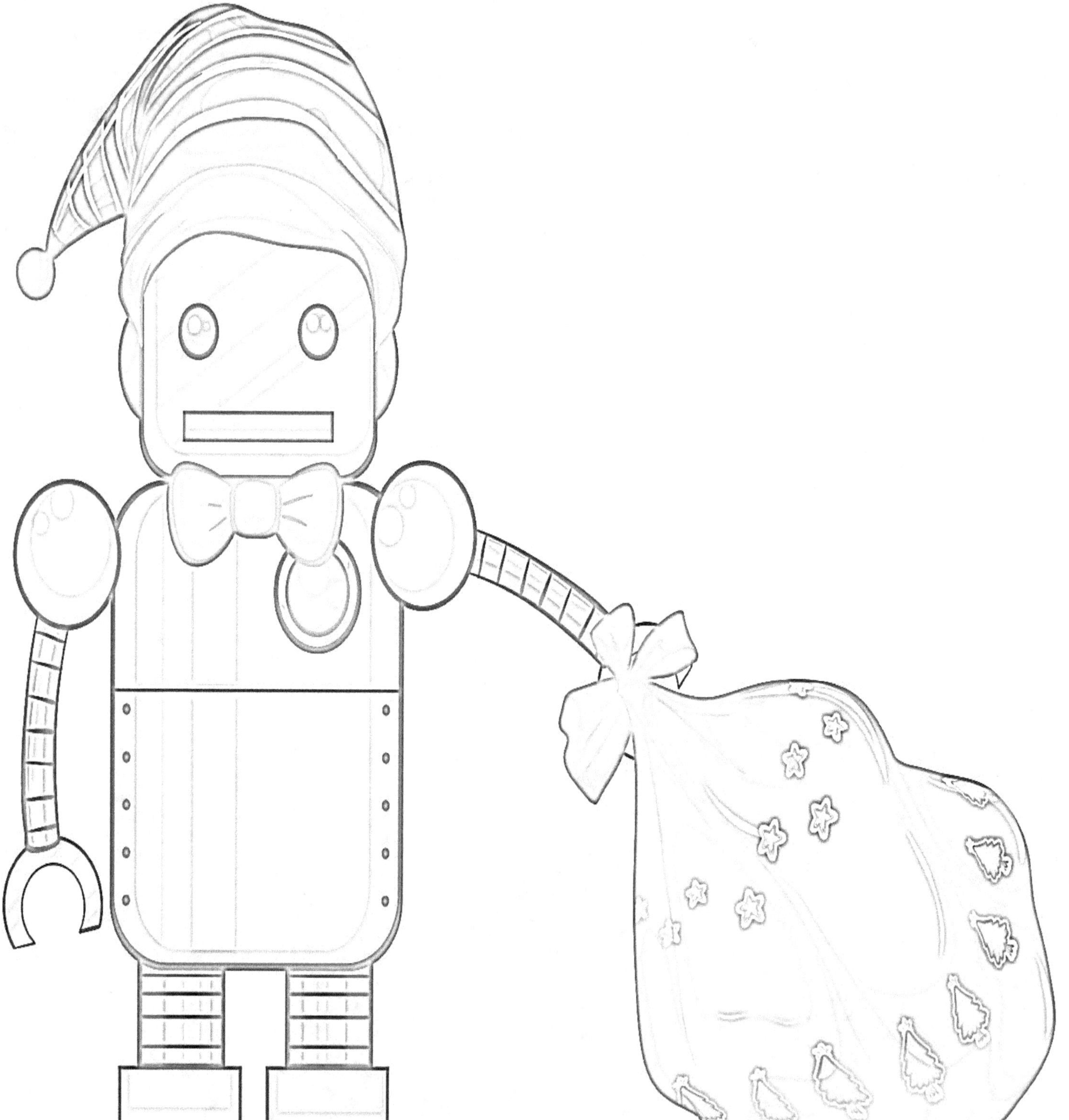

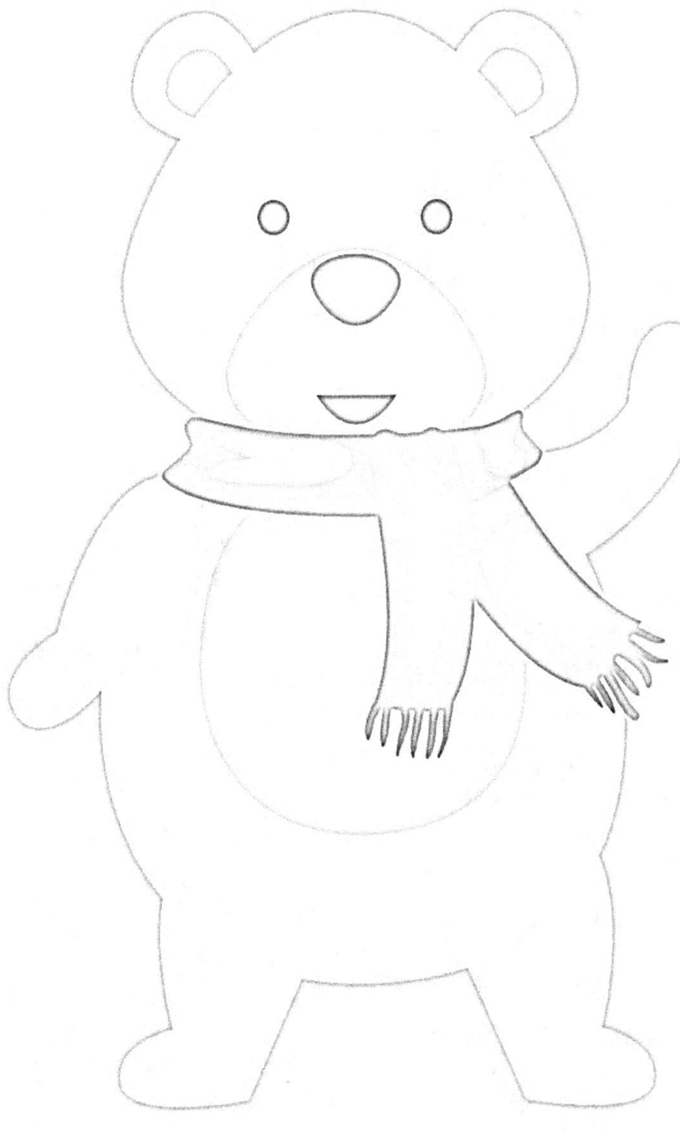

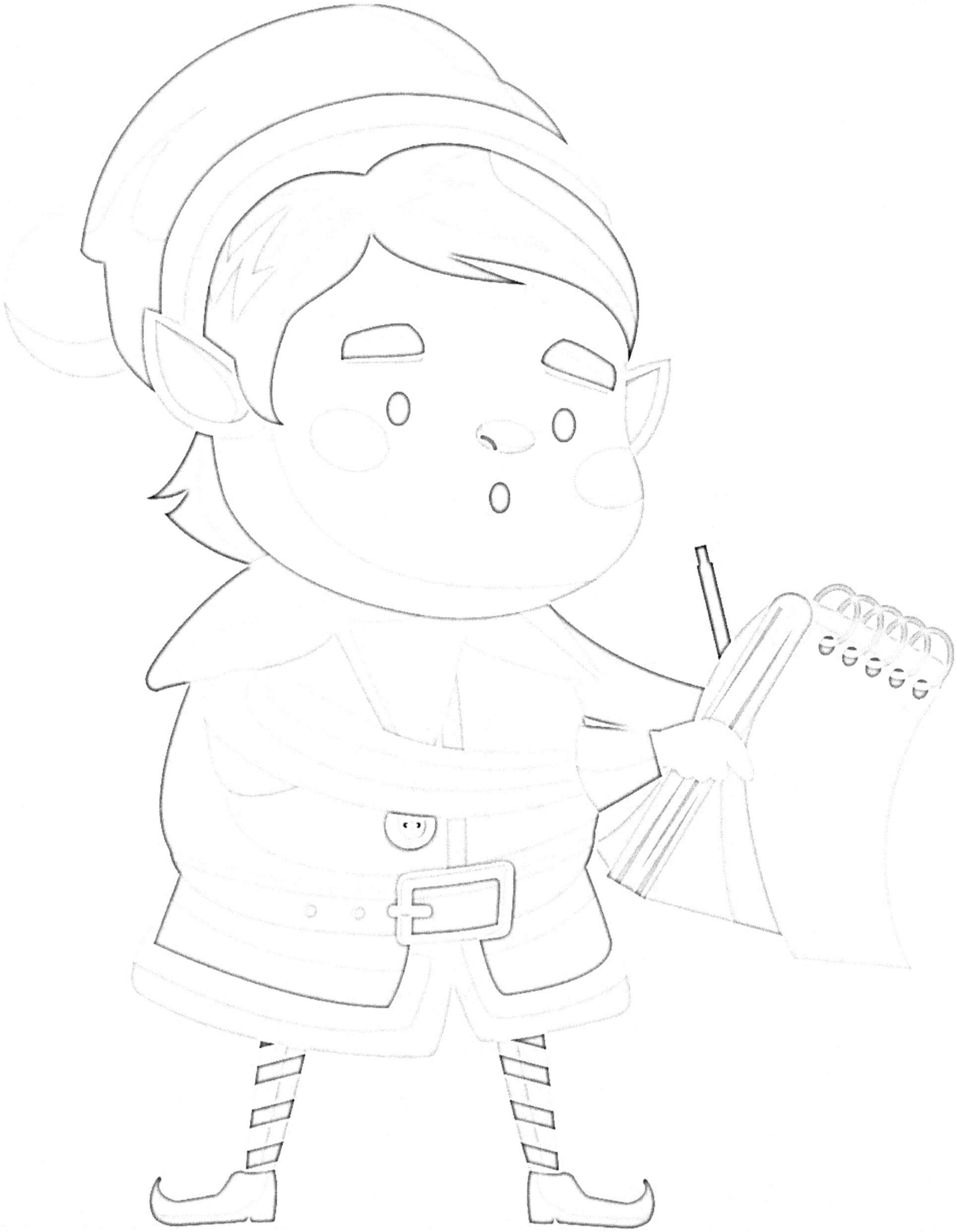

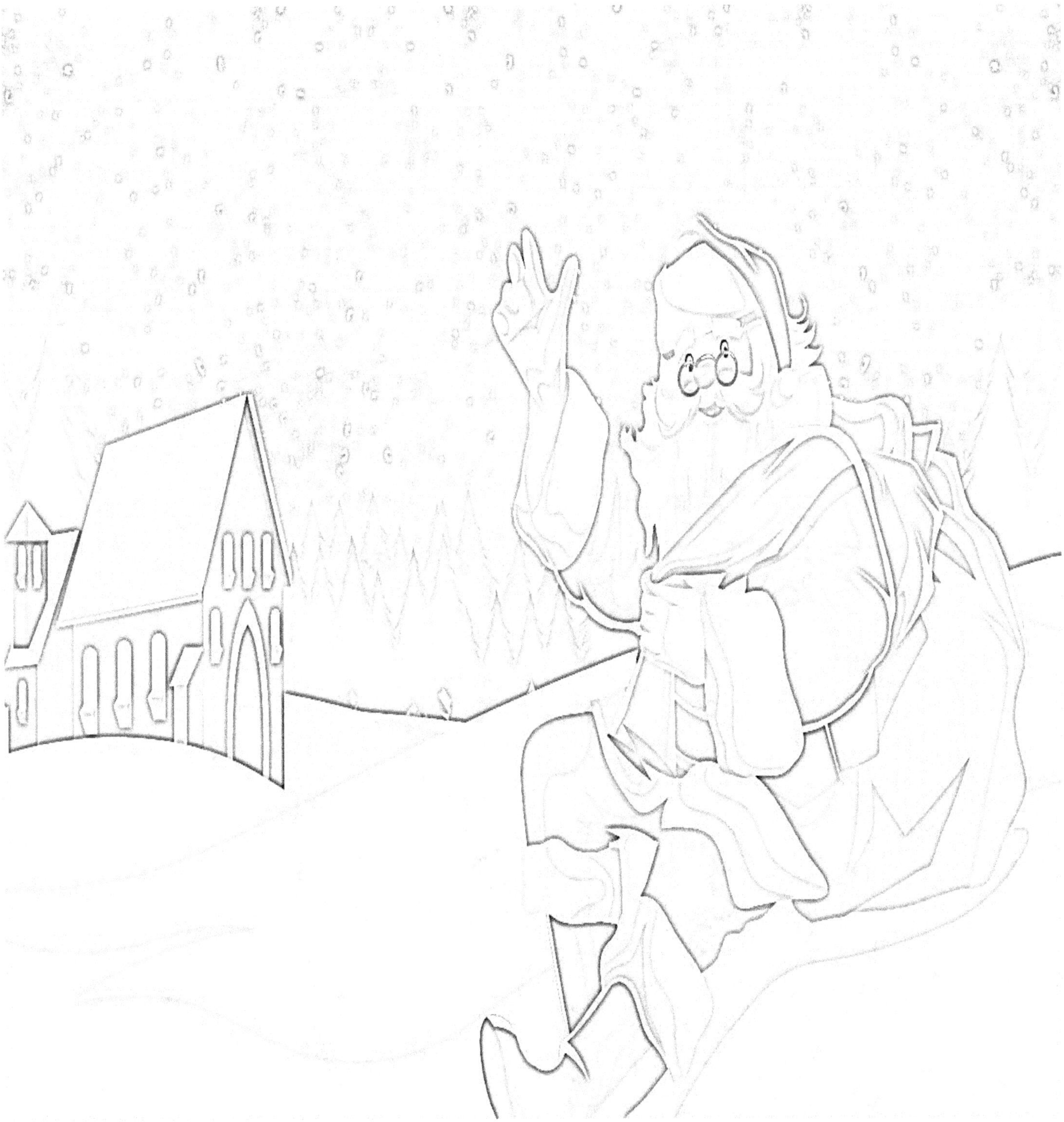

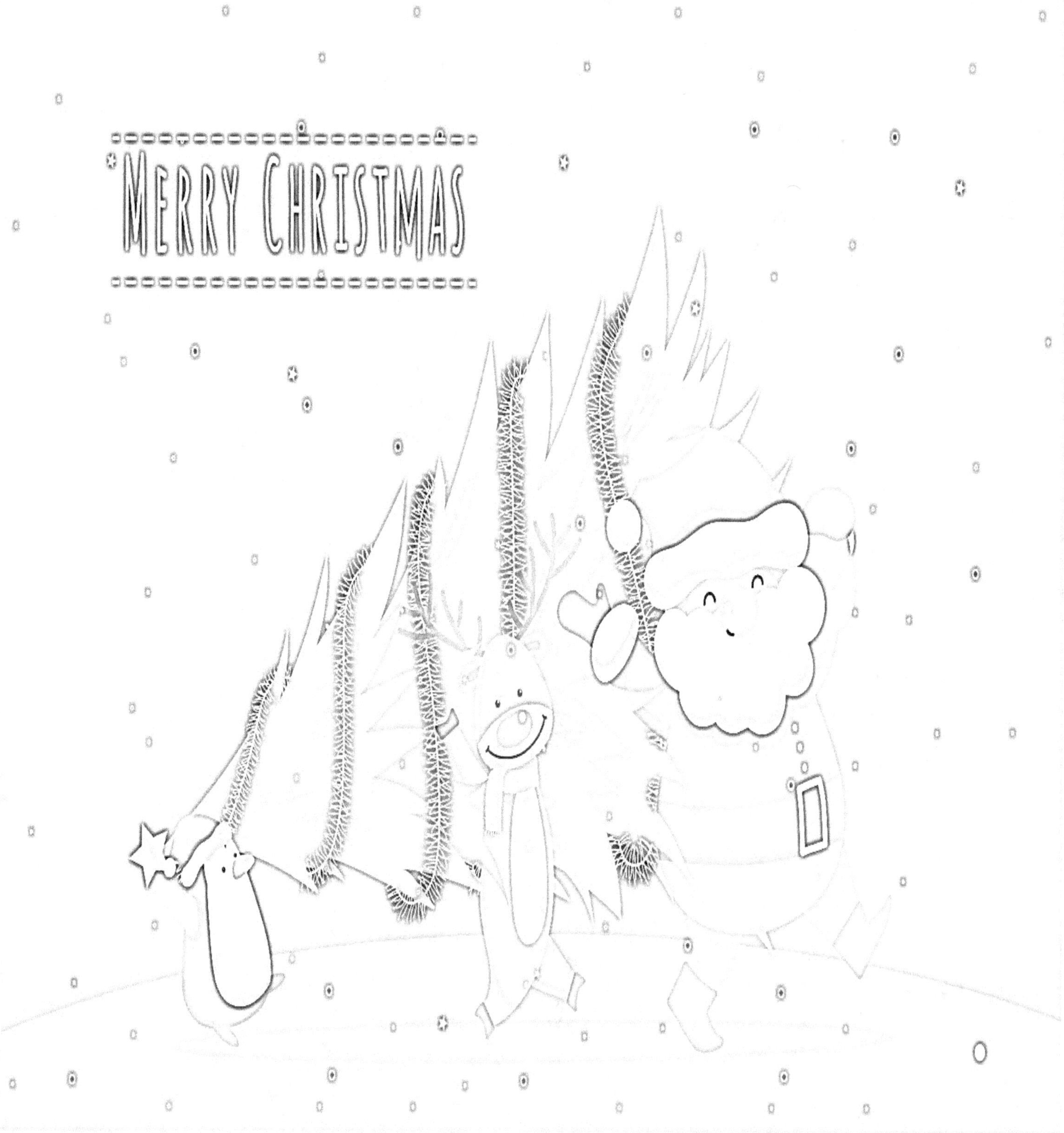
MERRY CHRISTMAS

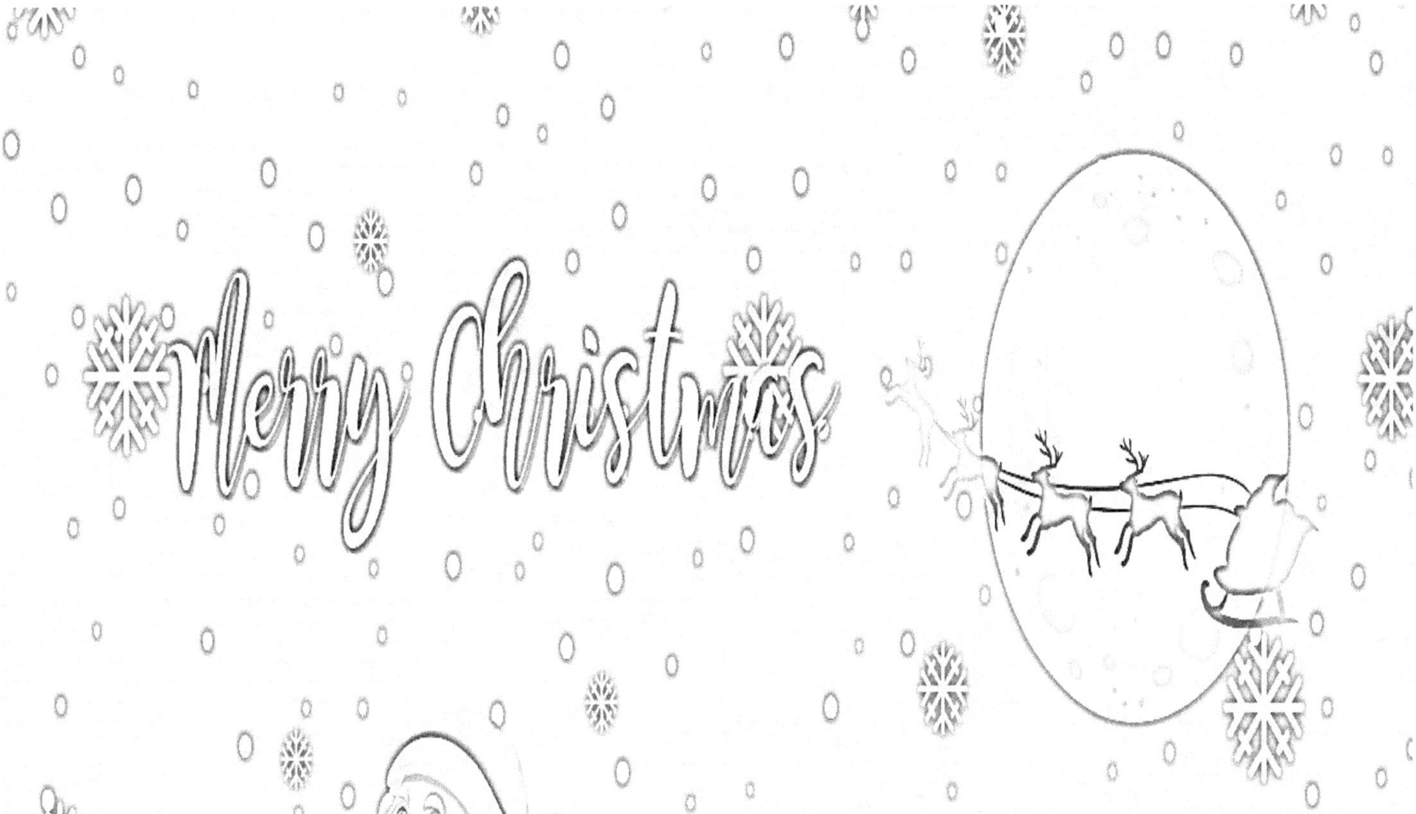
Merry Christmas

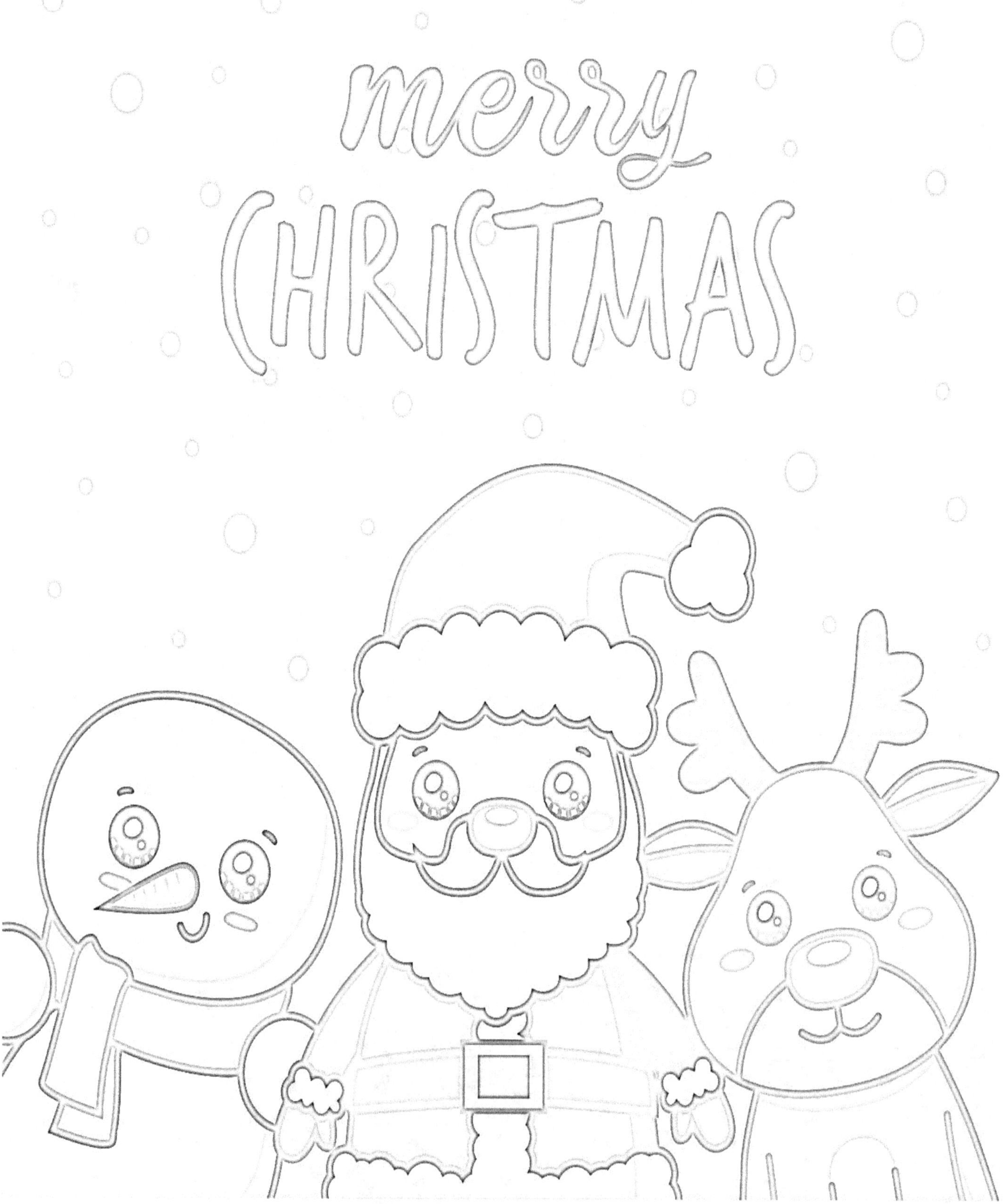
merry
CHRISTMAS

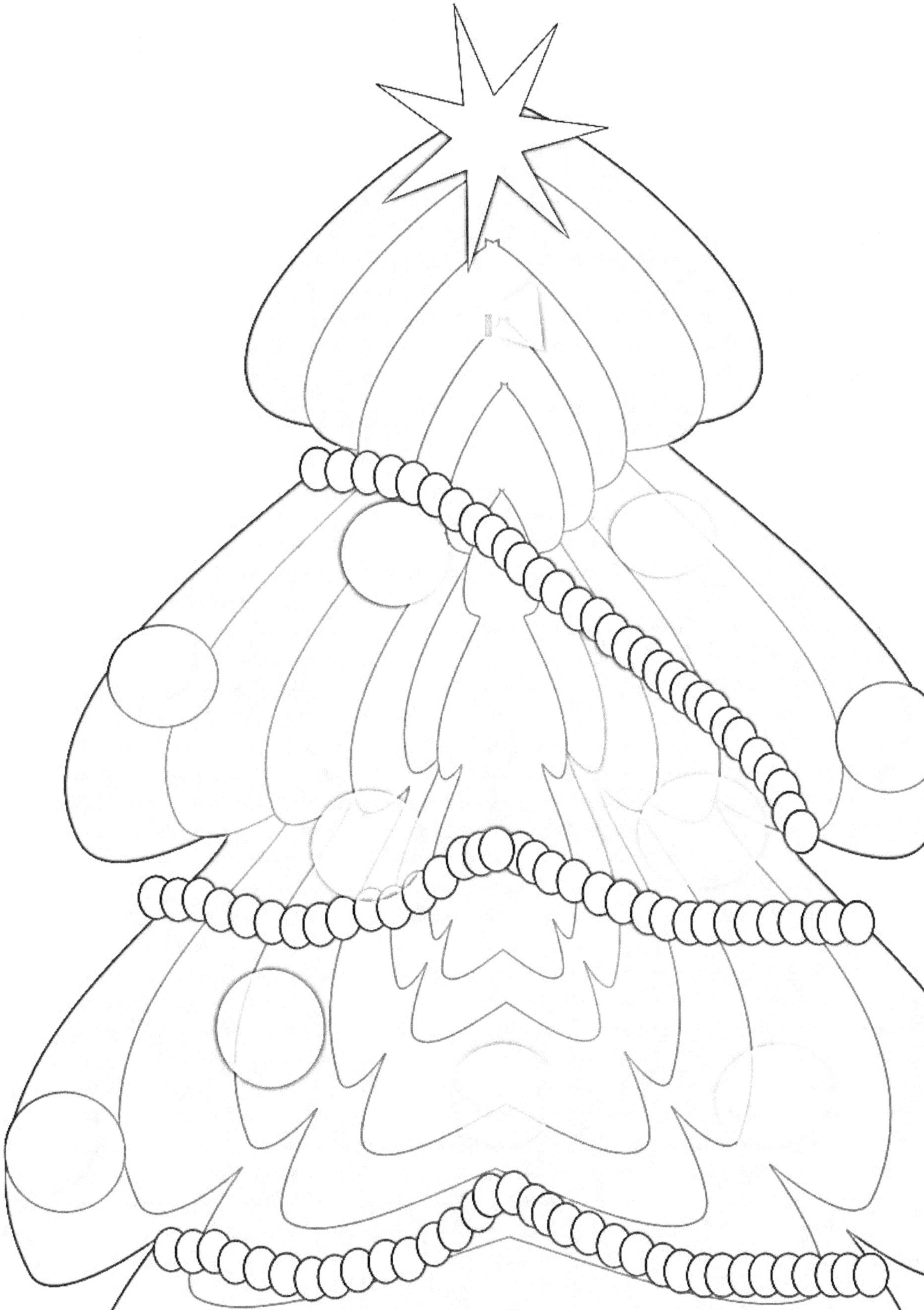

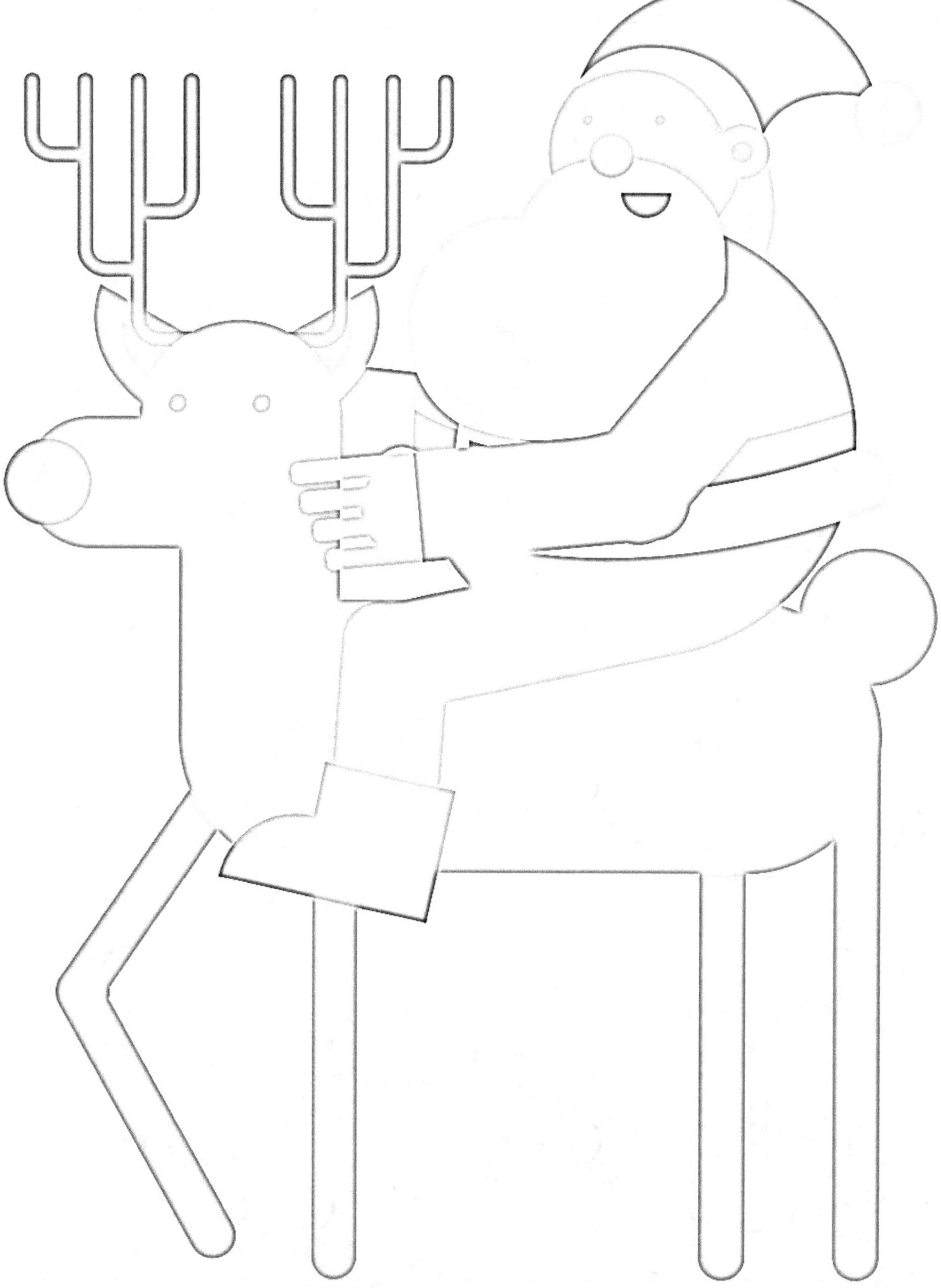

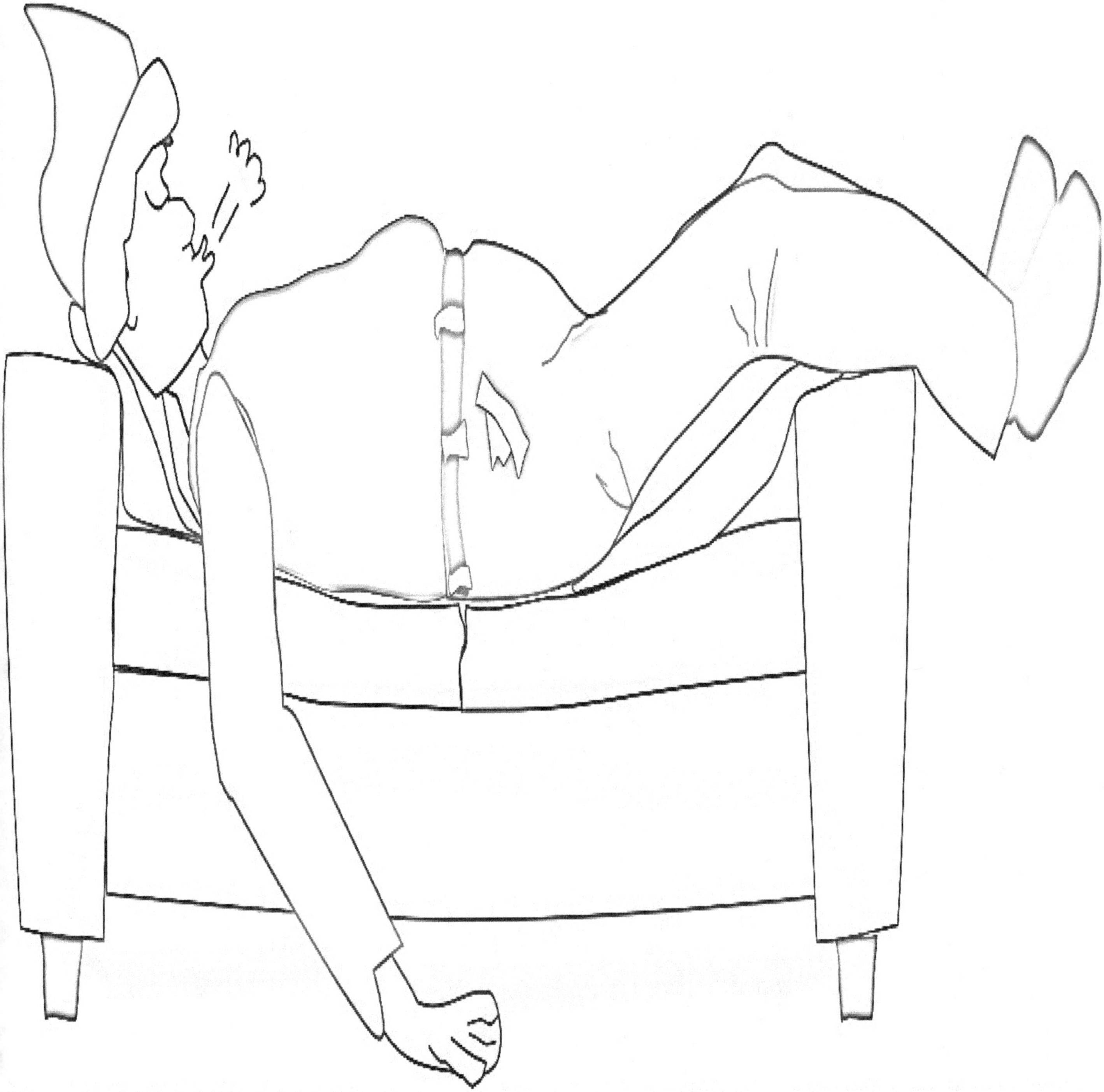

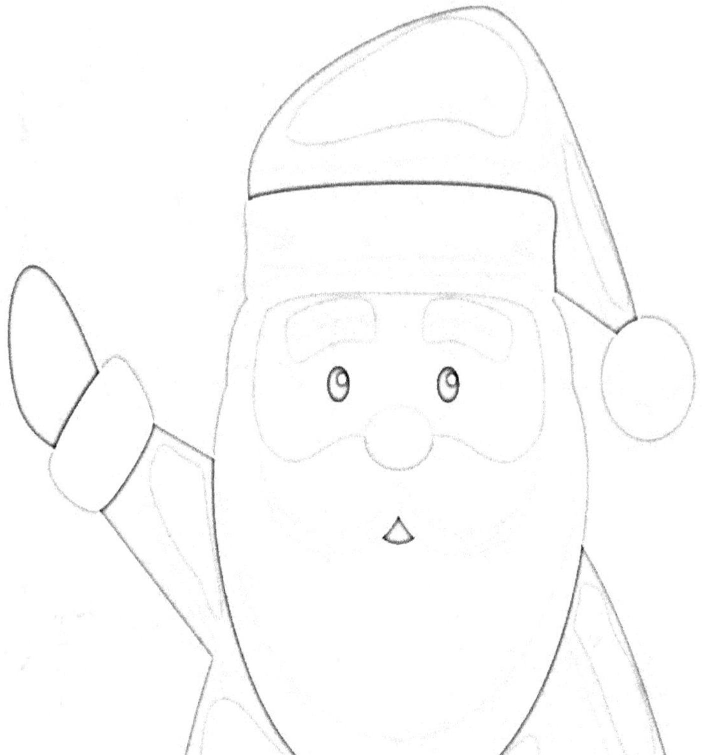

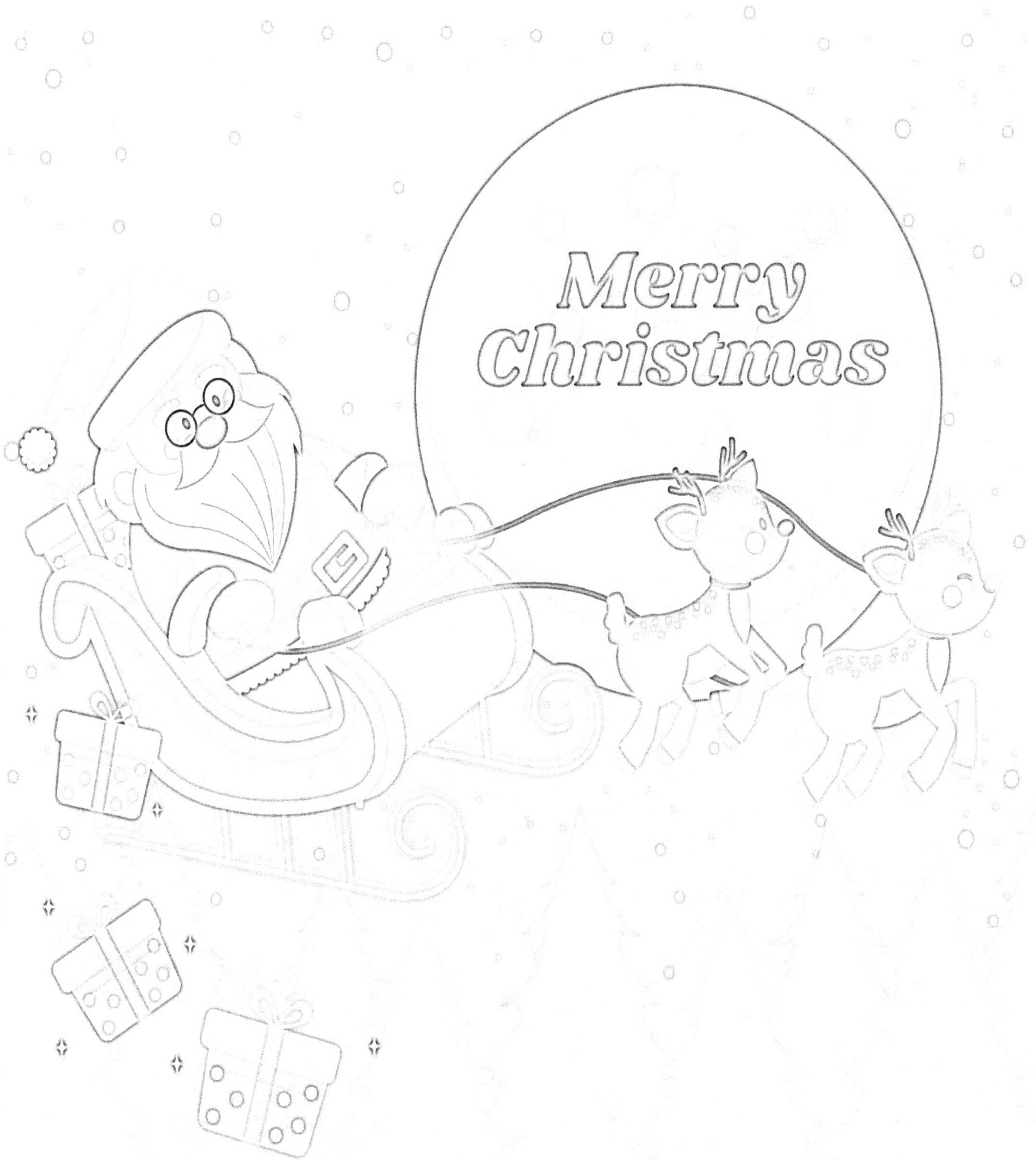
Merry
Christmas

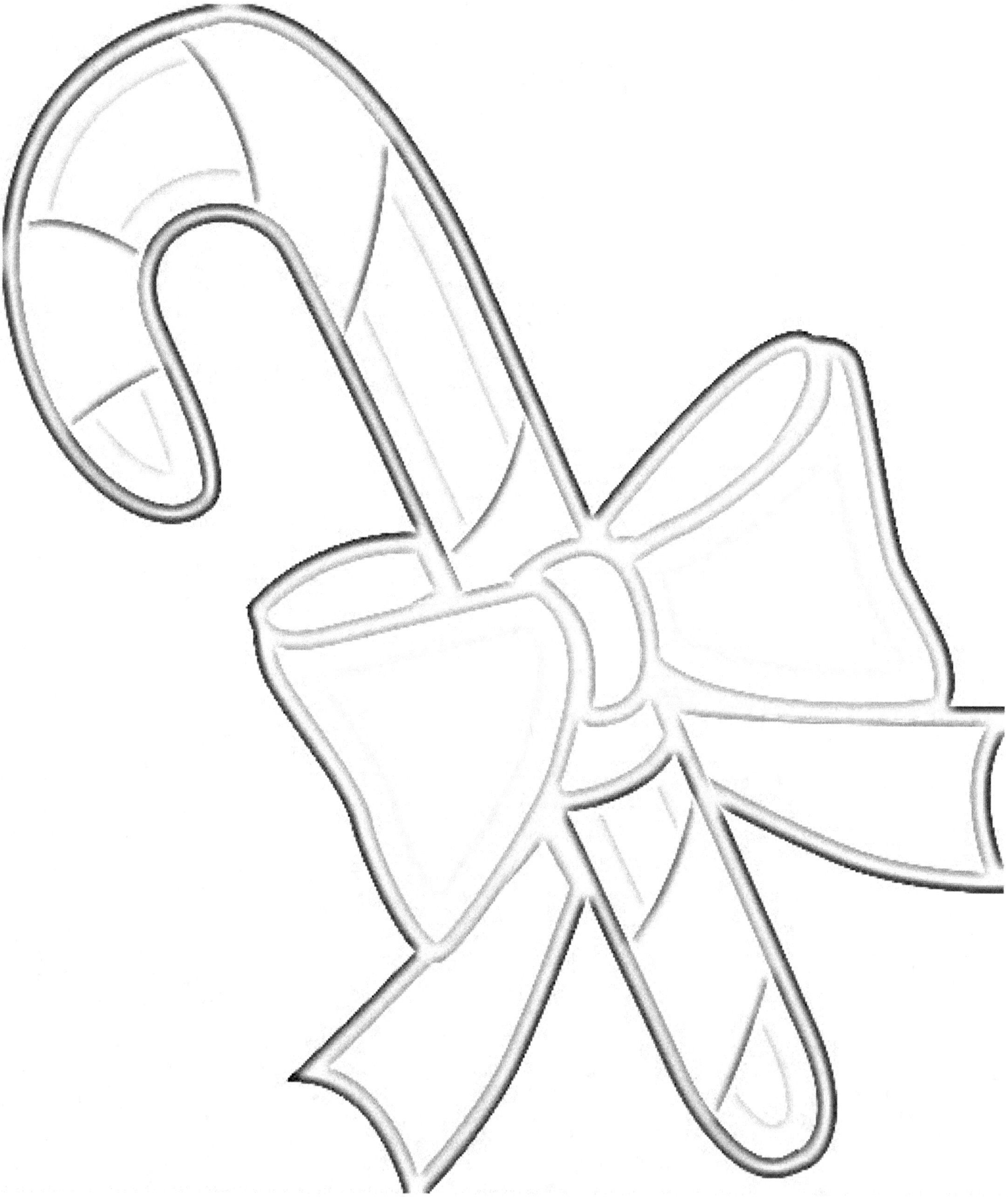

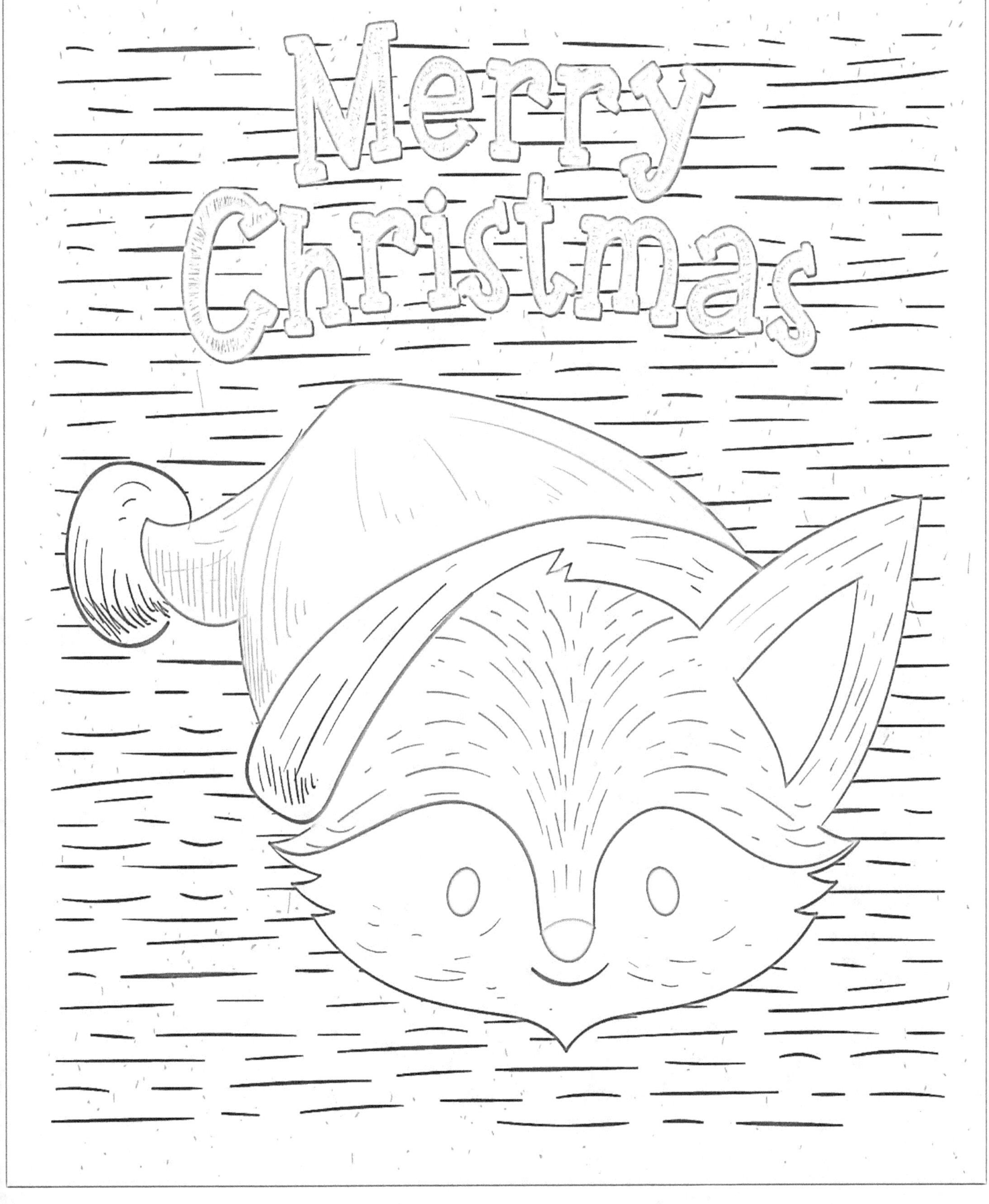
Merry Christmas

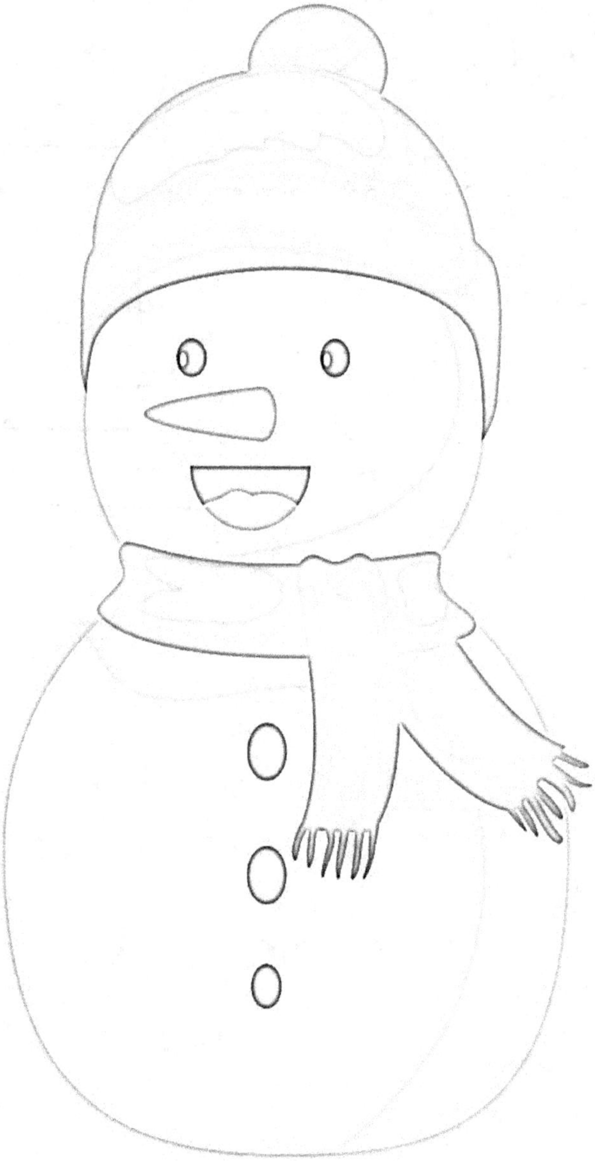

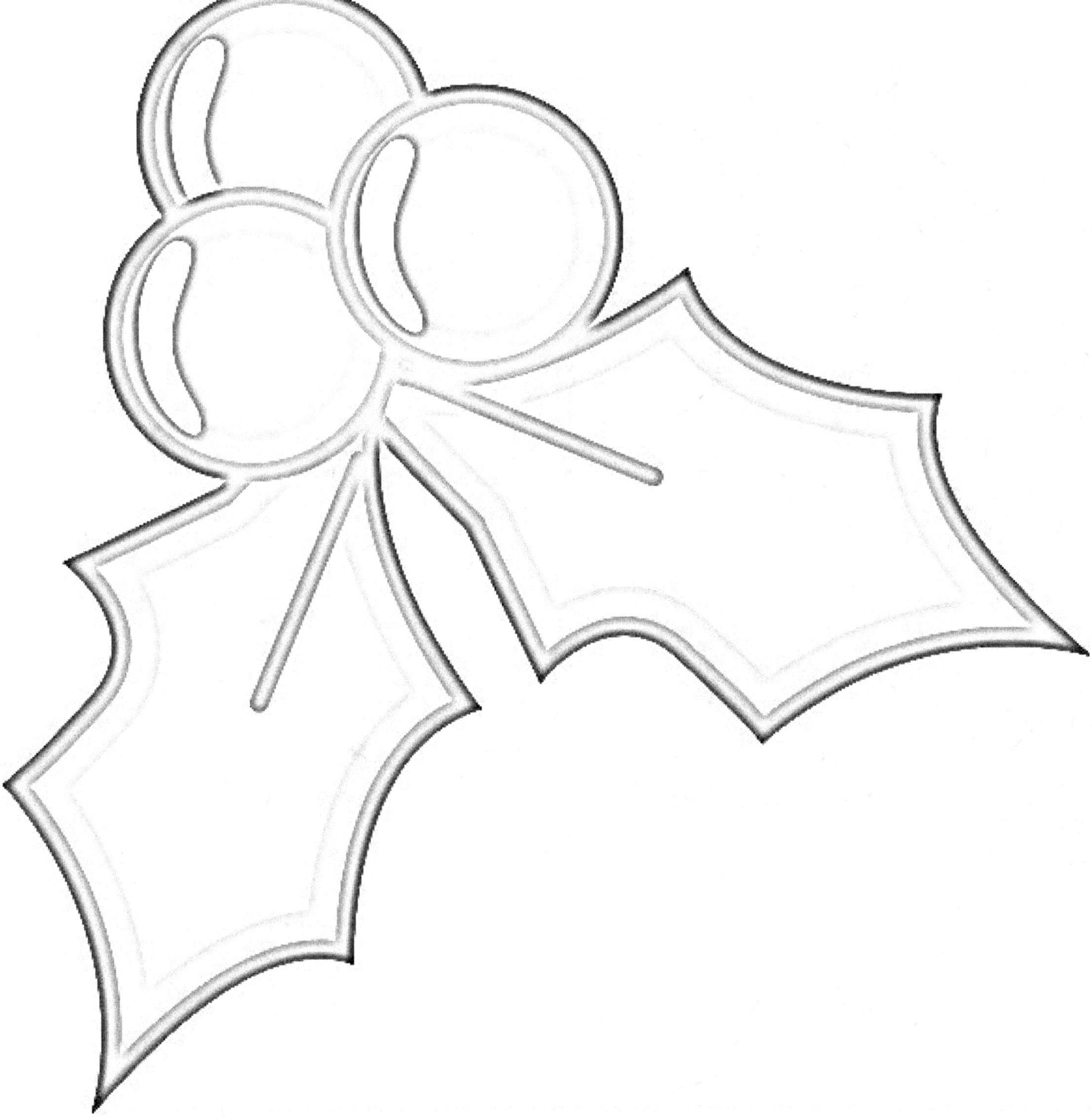

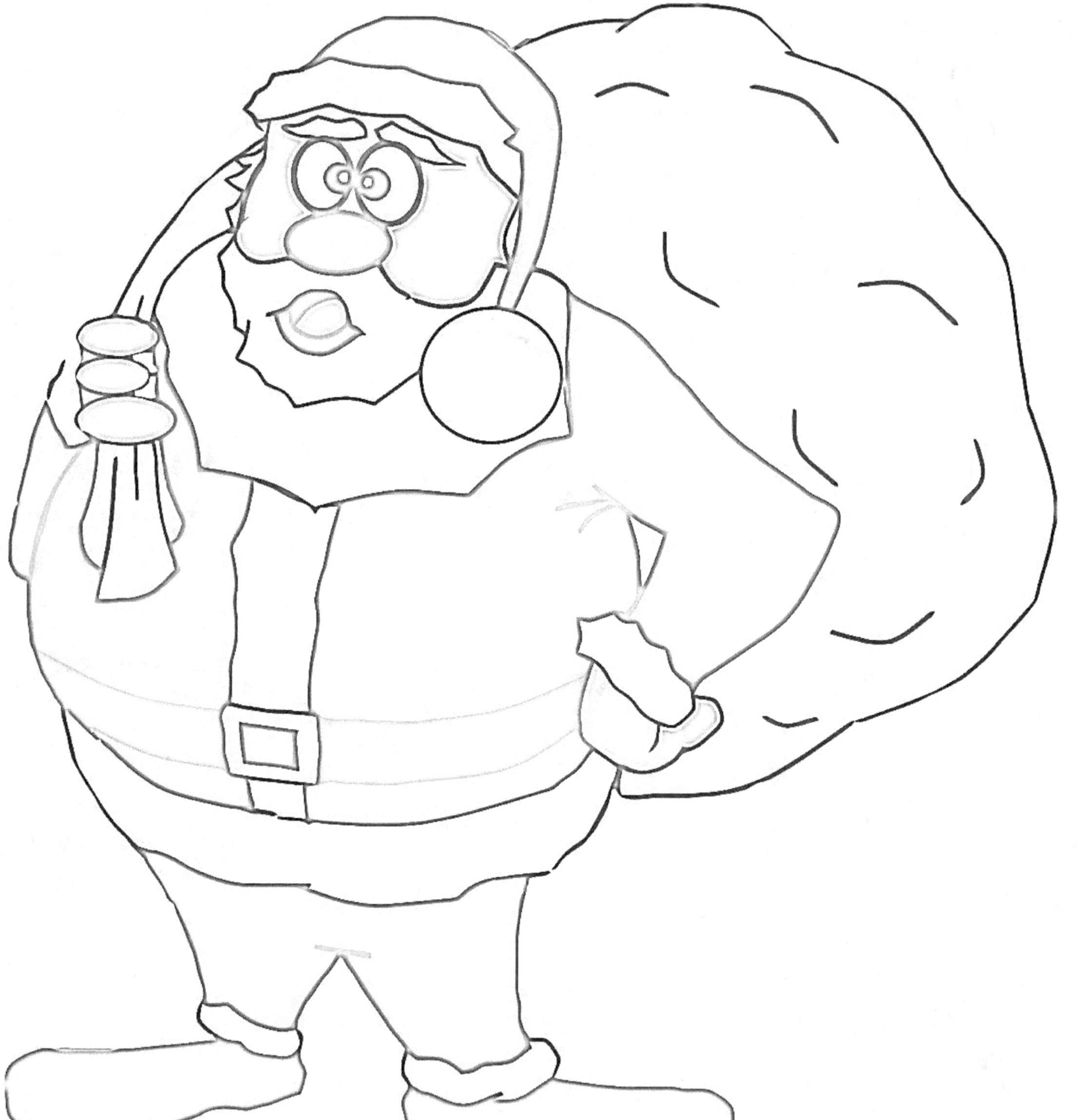

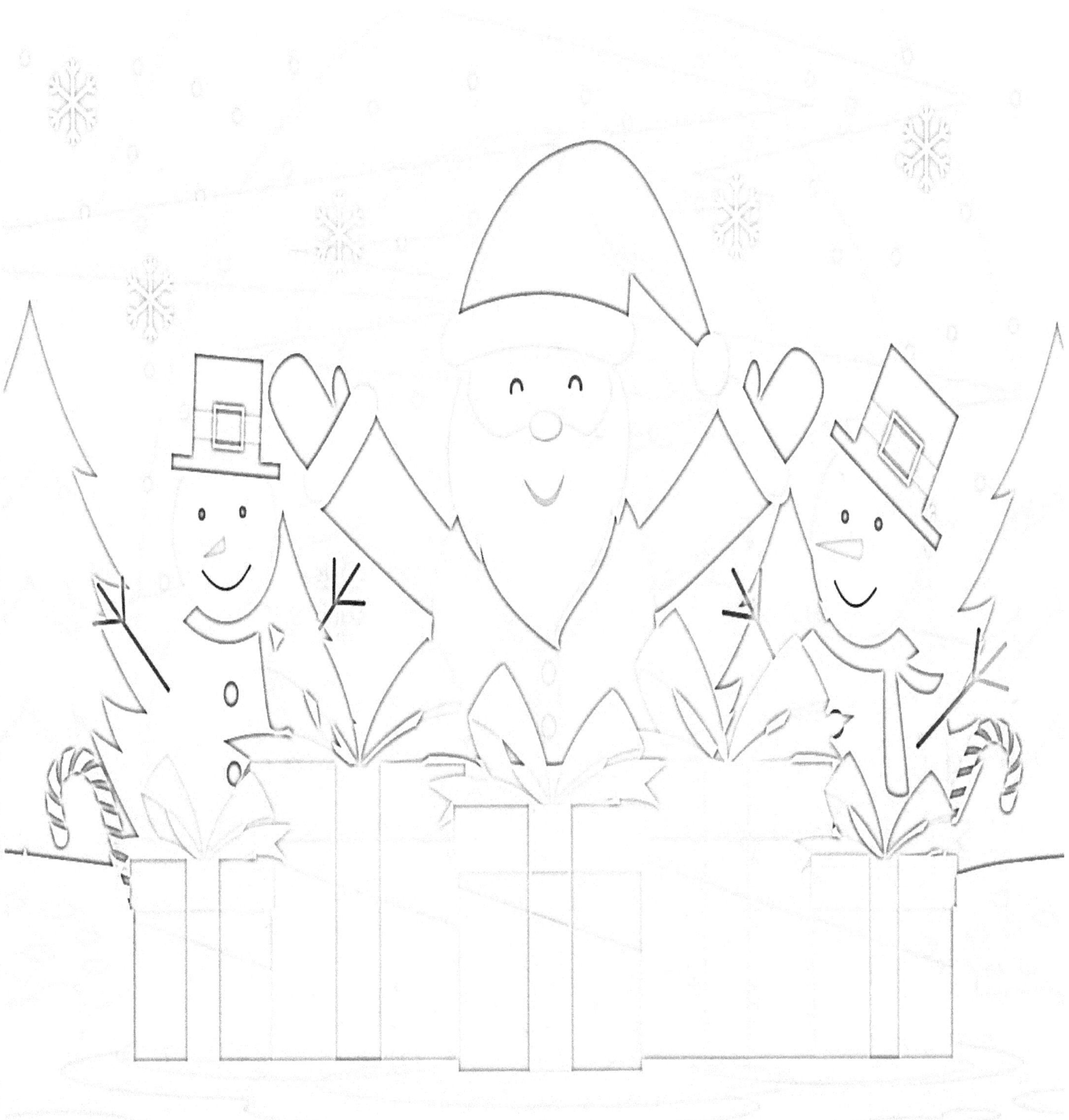

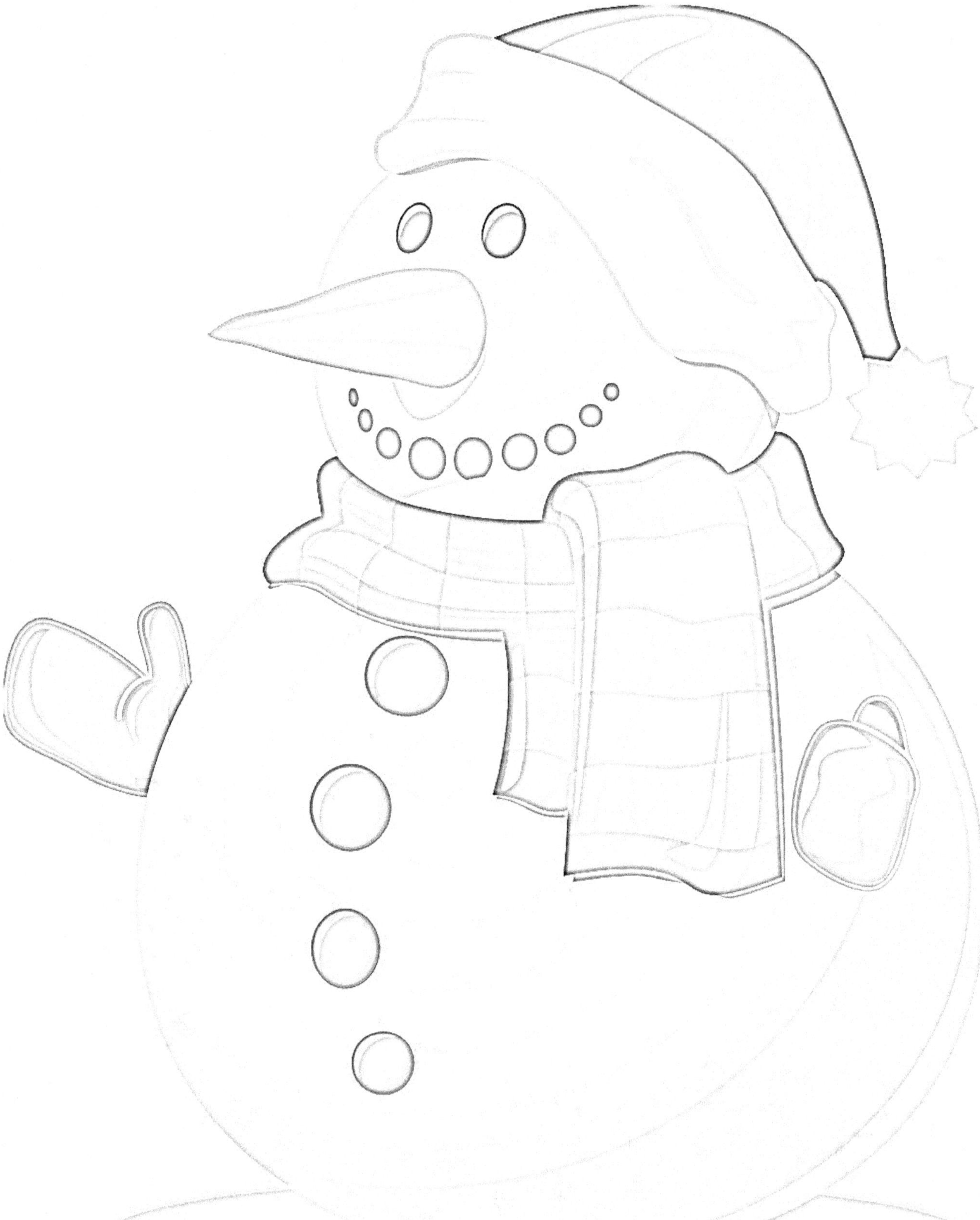

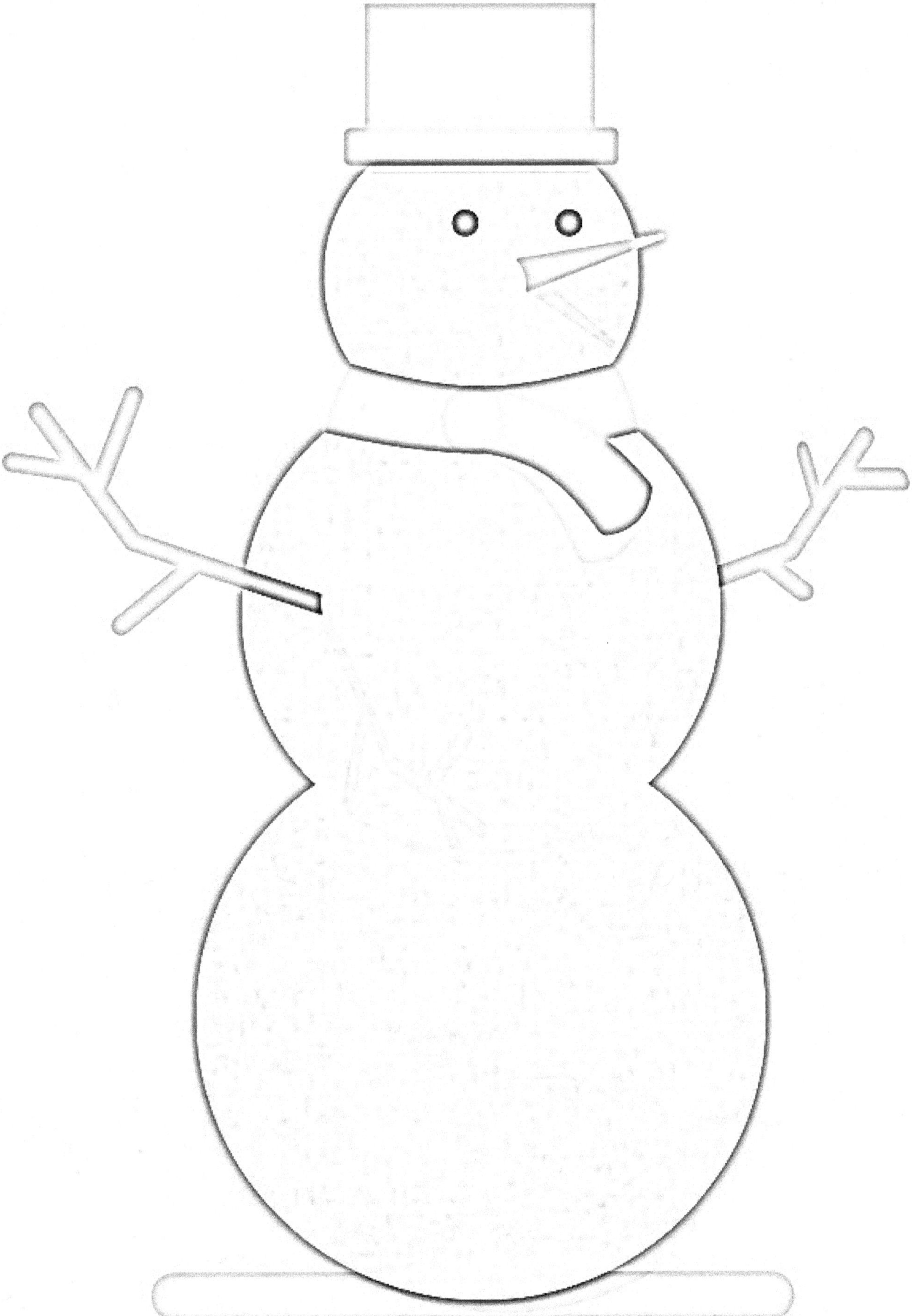

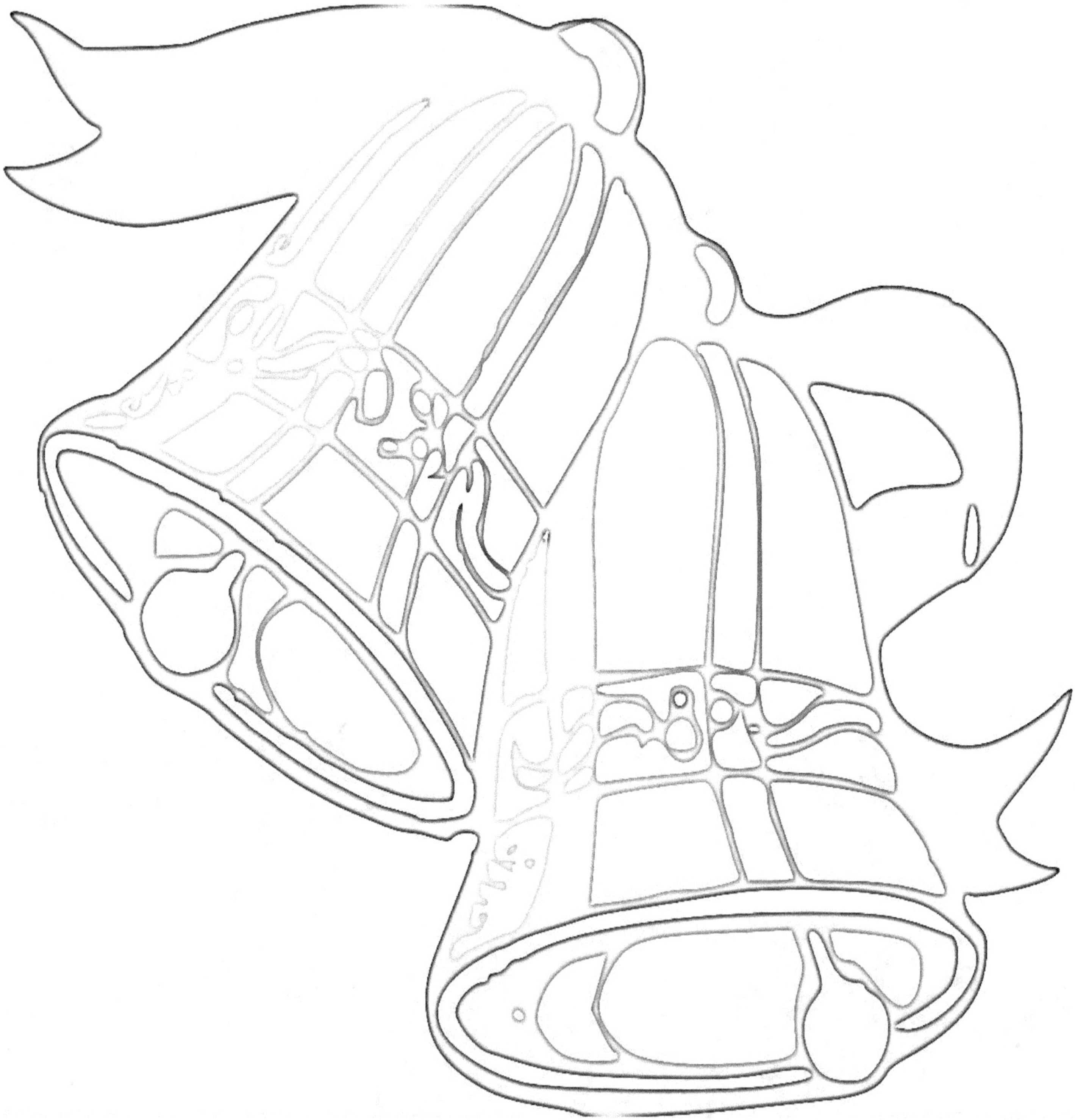

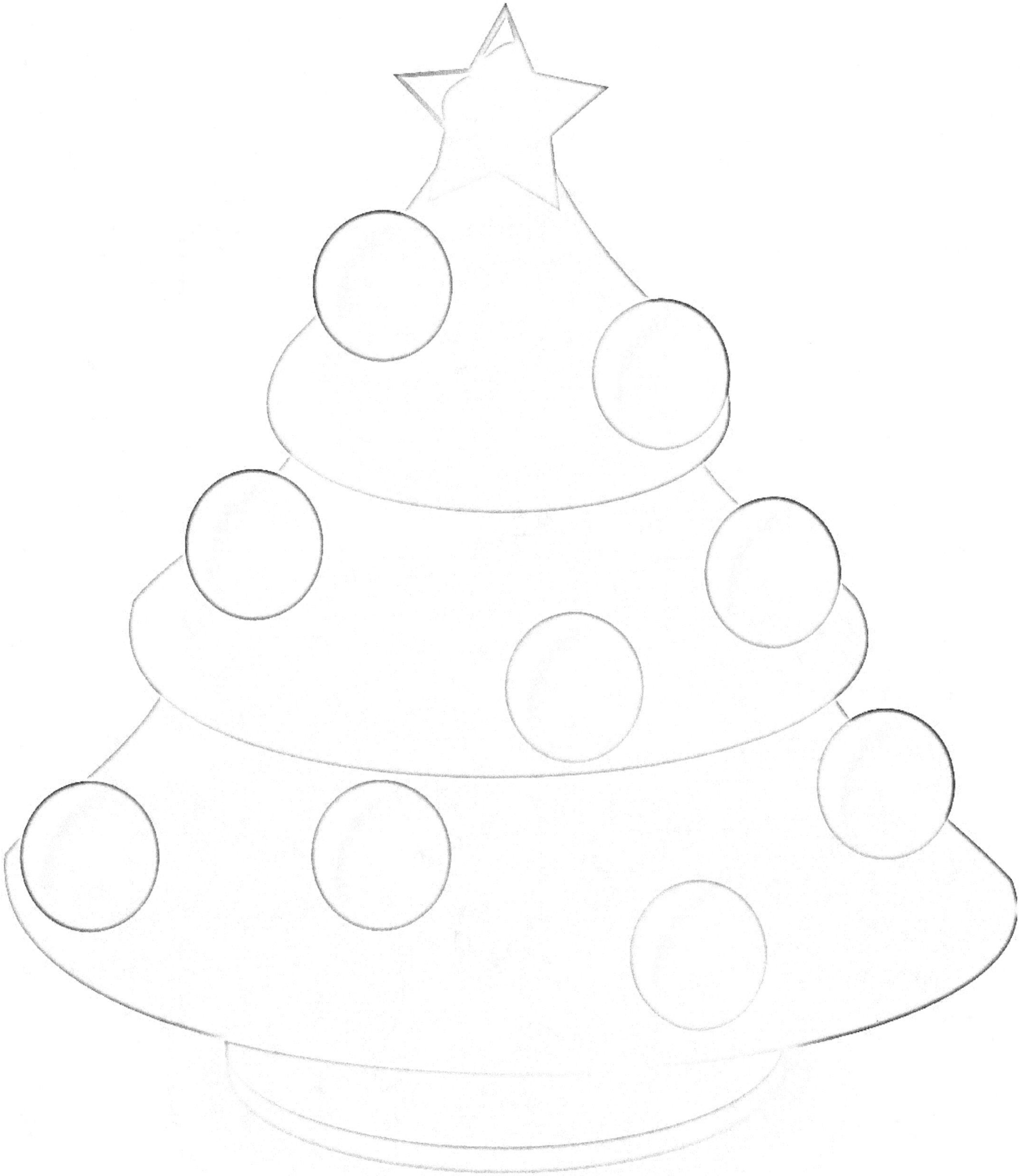

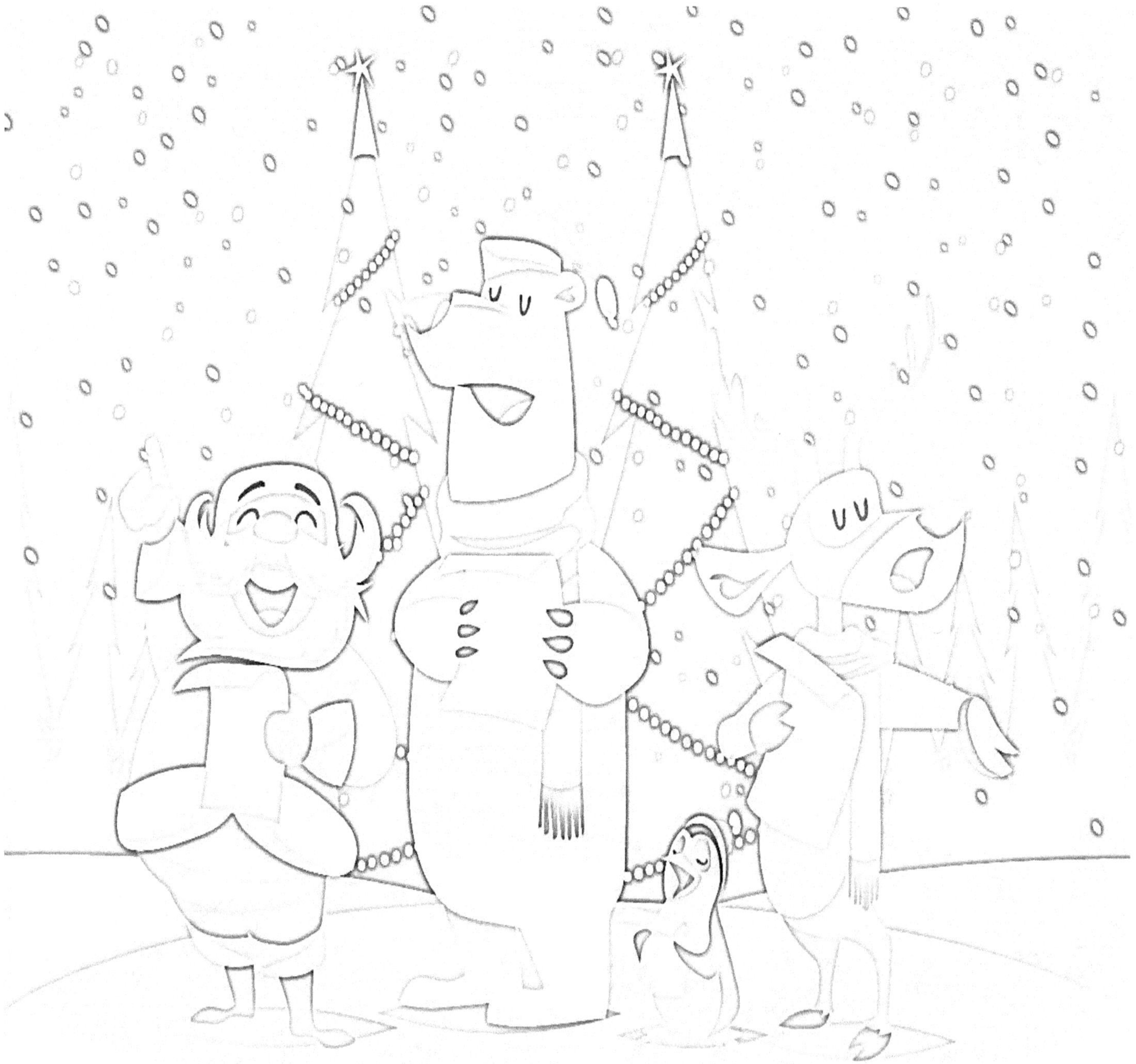

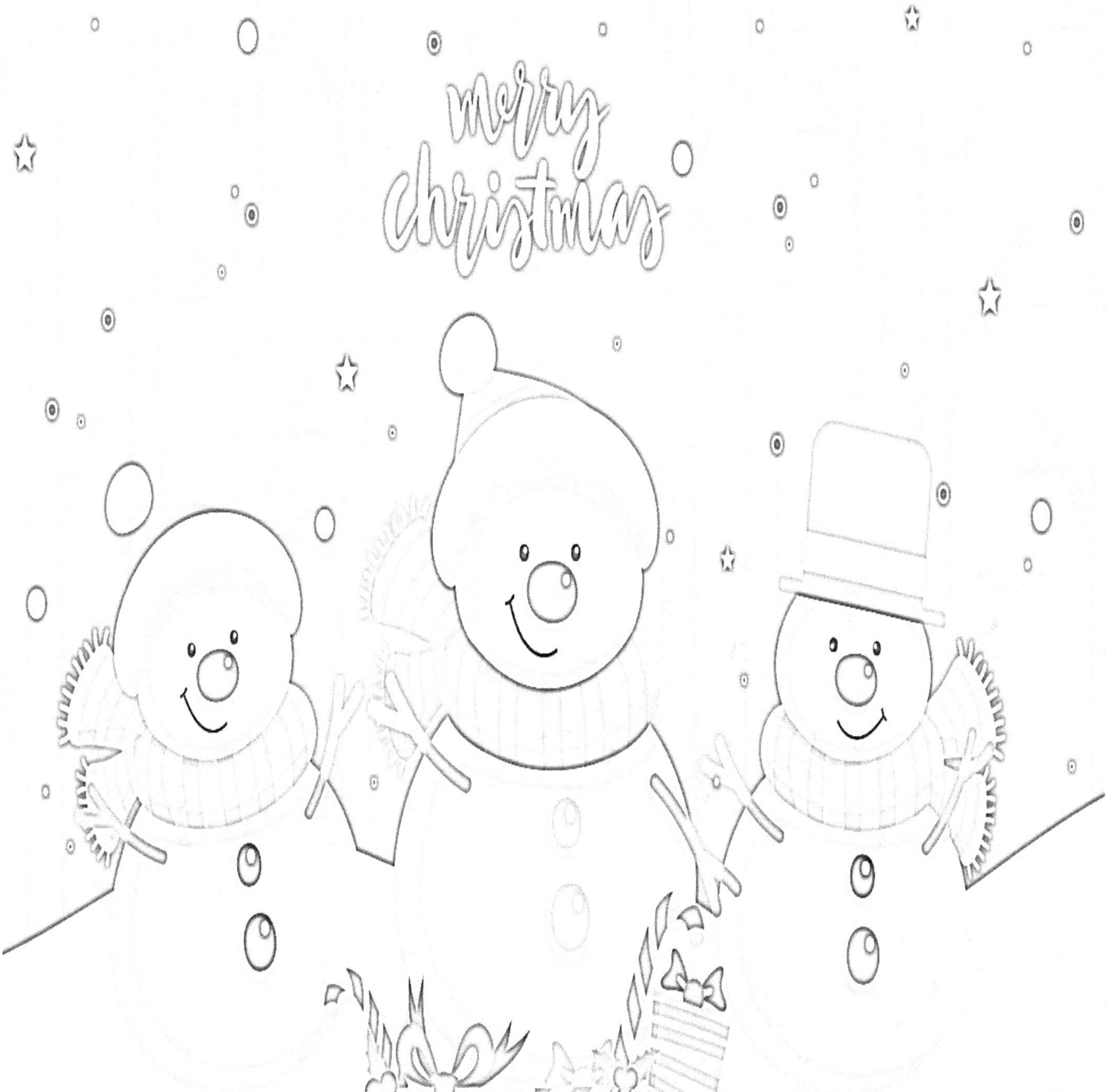
merry
christmas

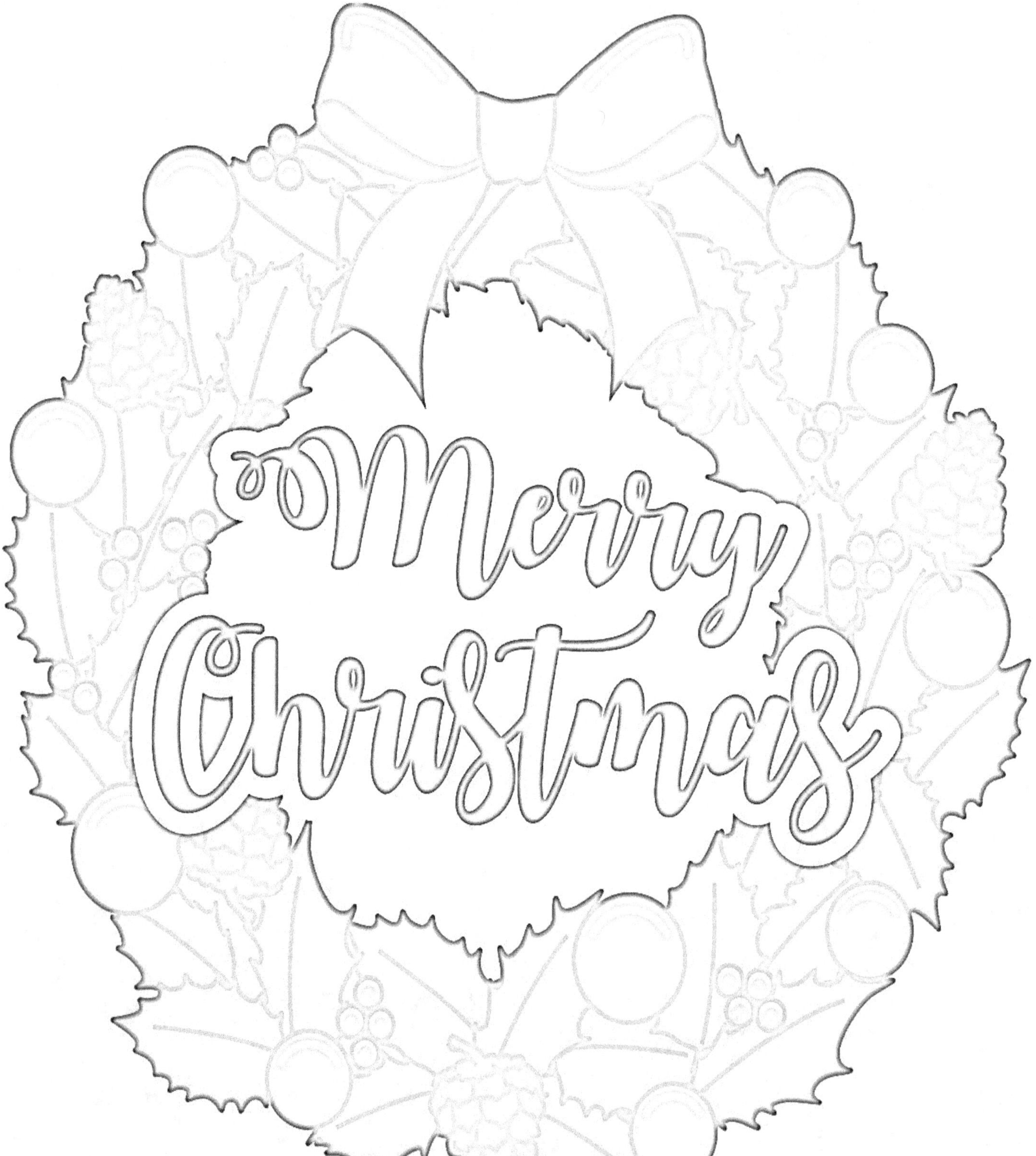
Merry
Christmas

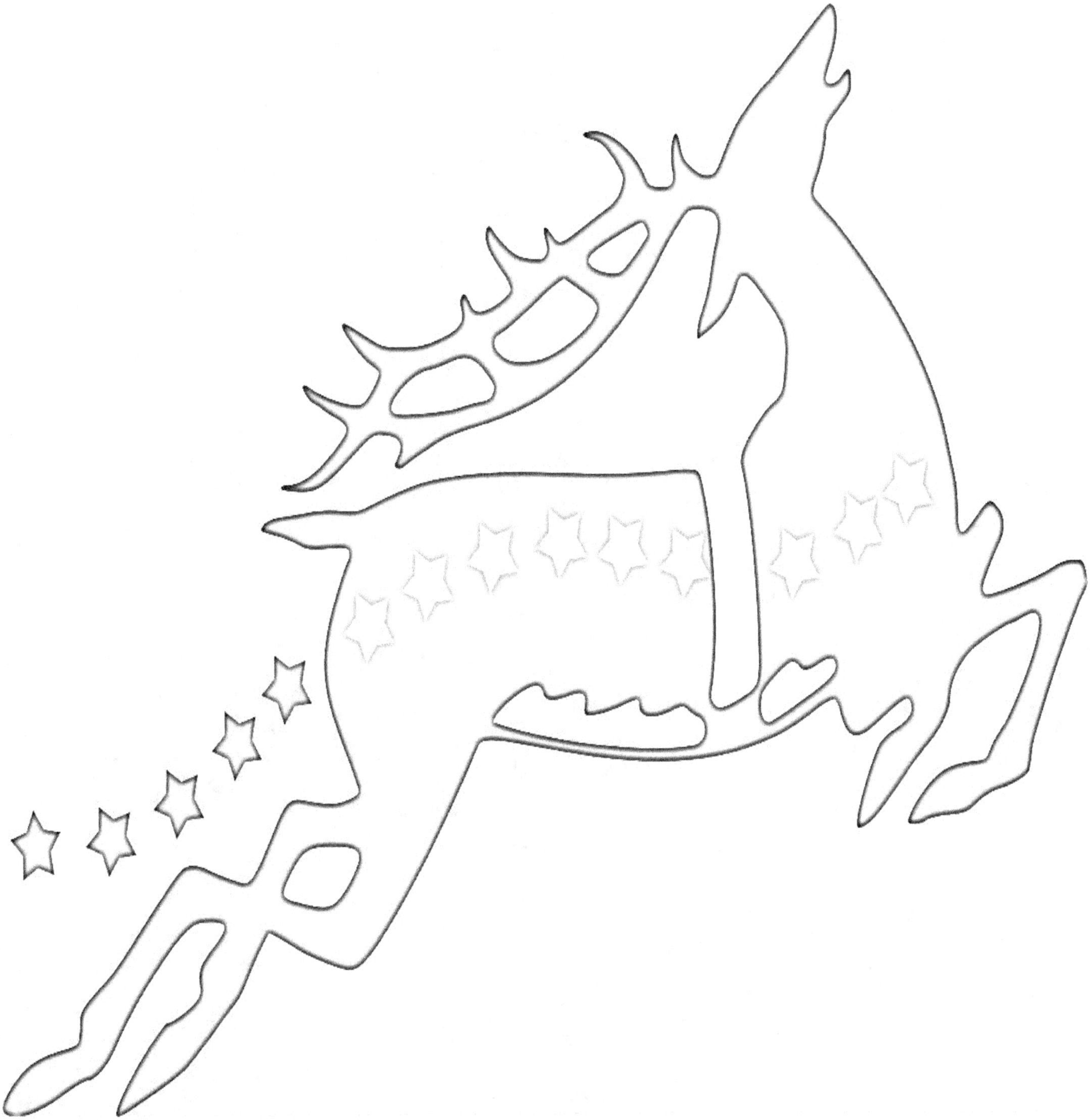

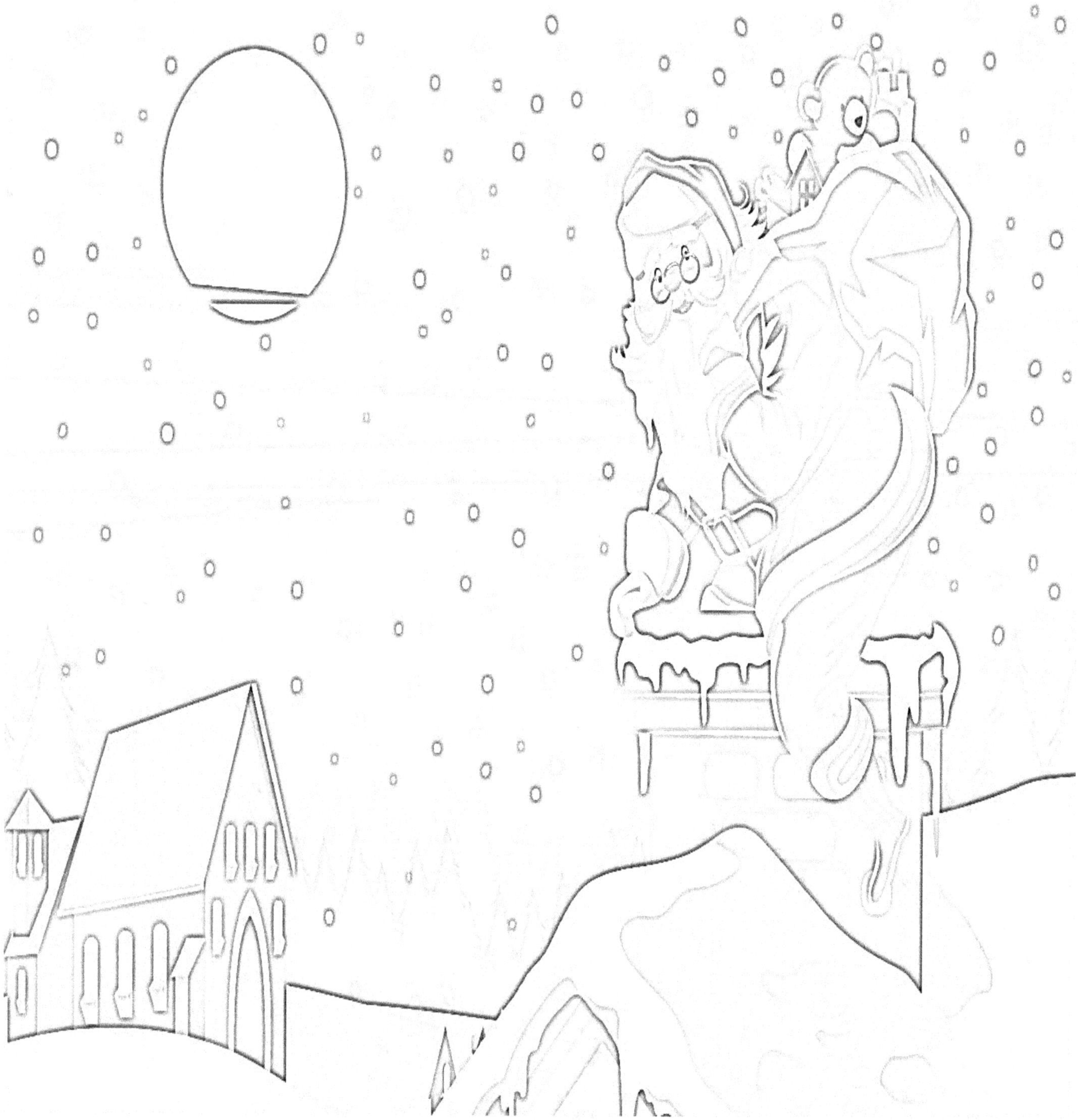

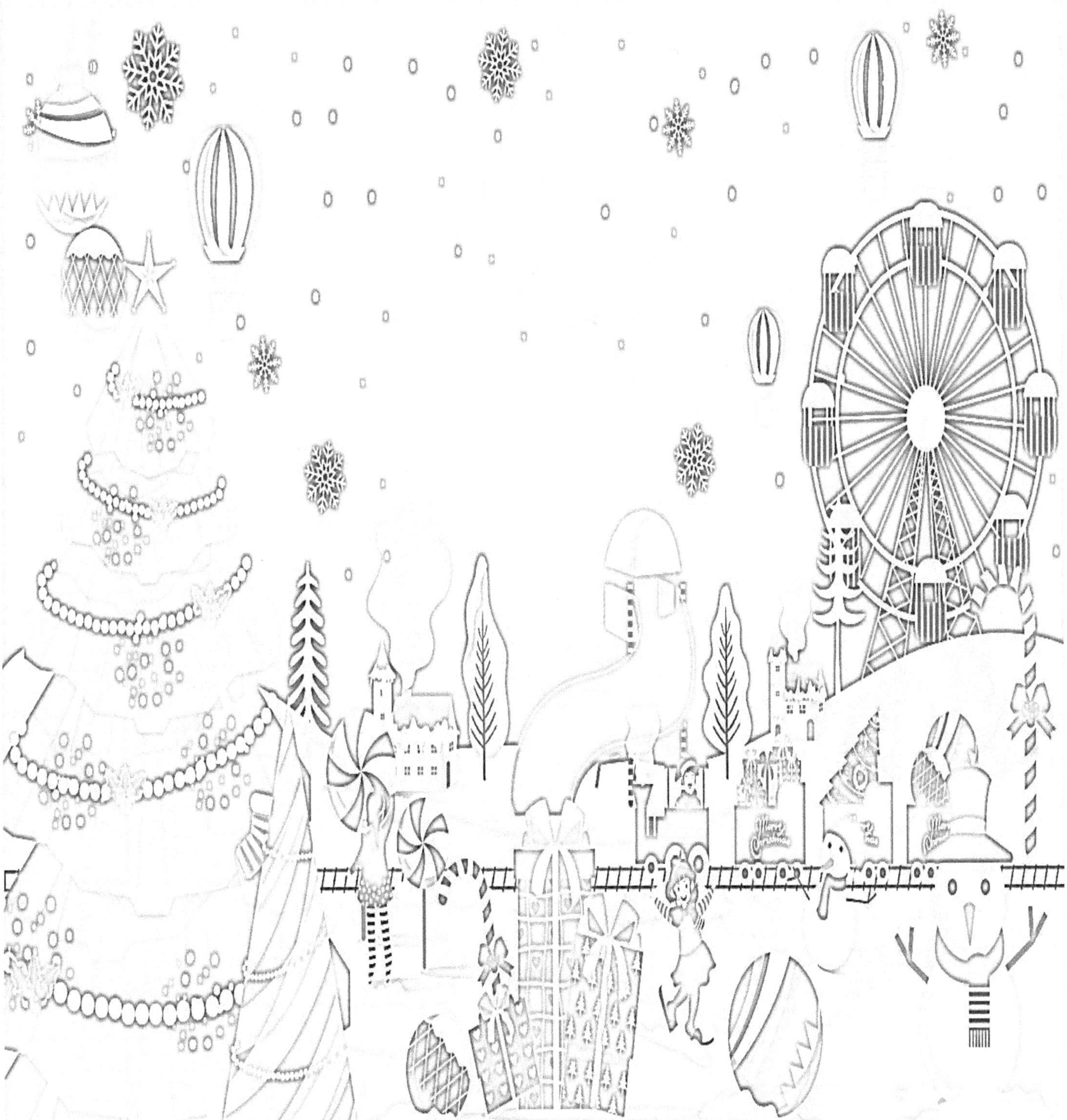

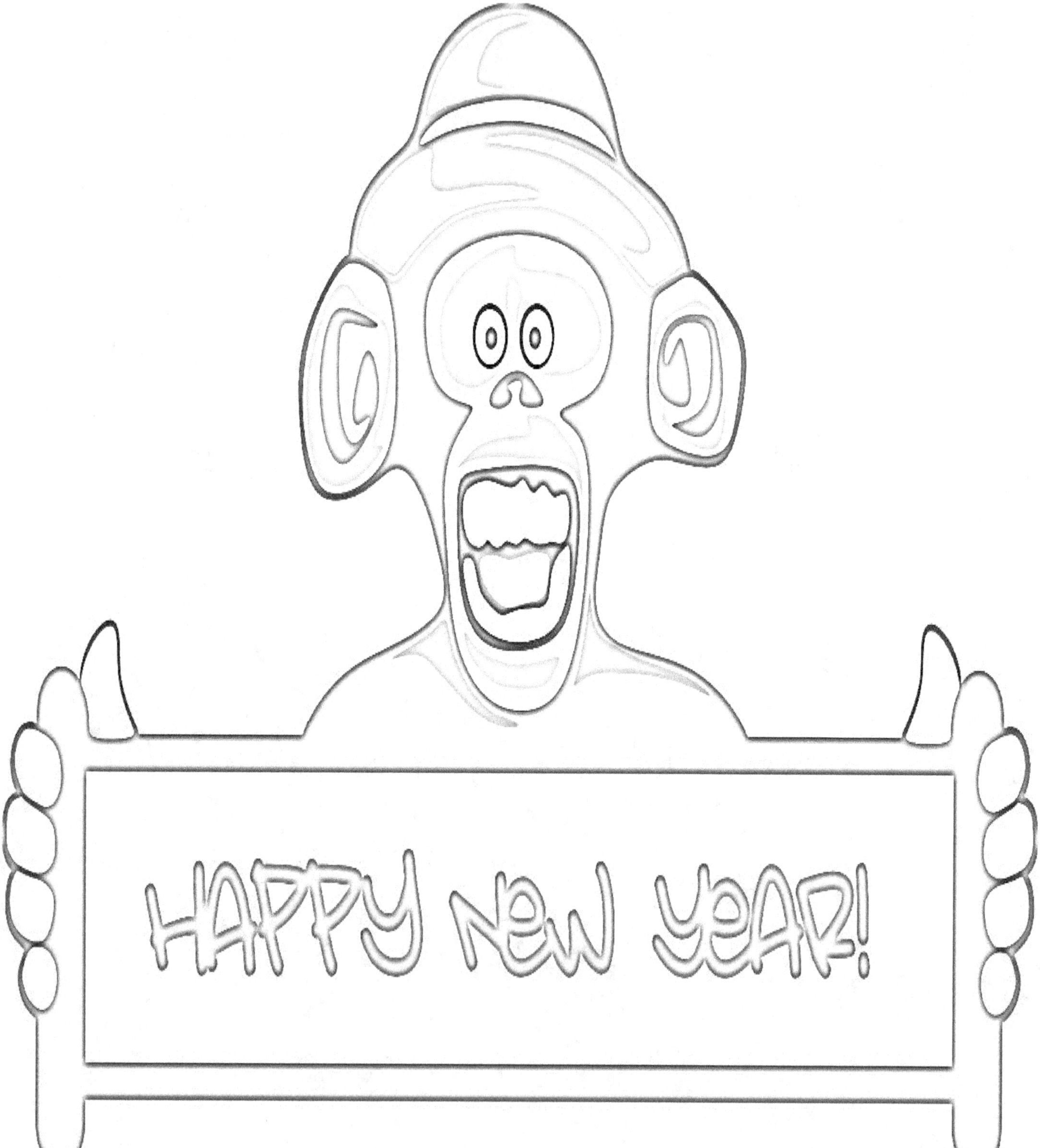
HAPPY NEW YEAR!

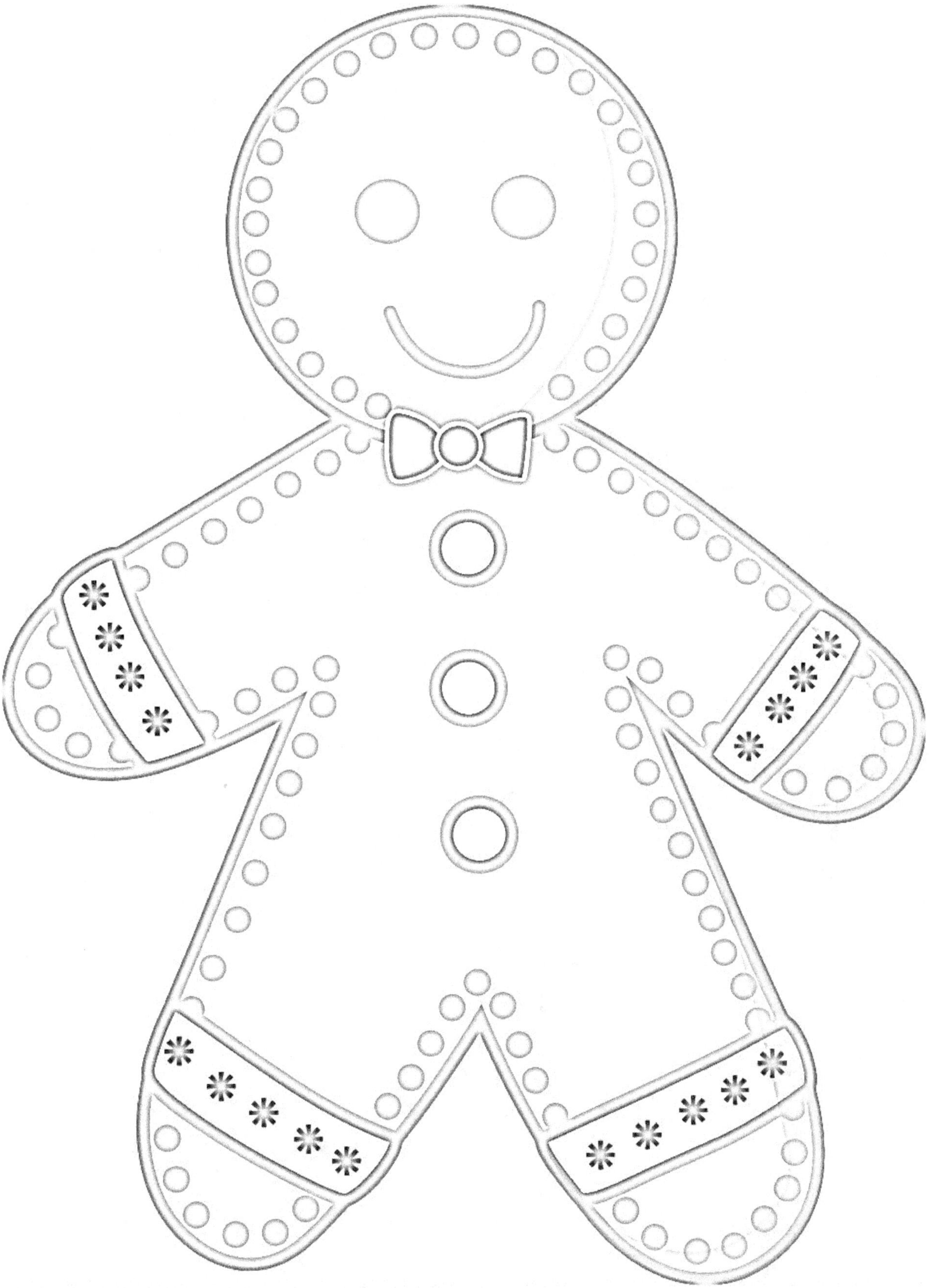

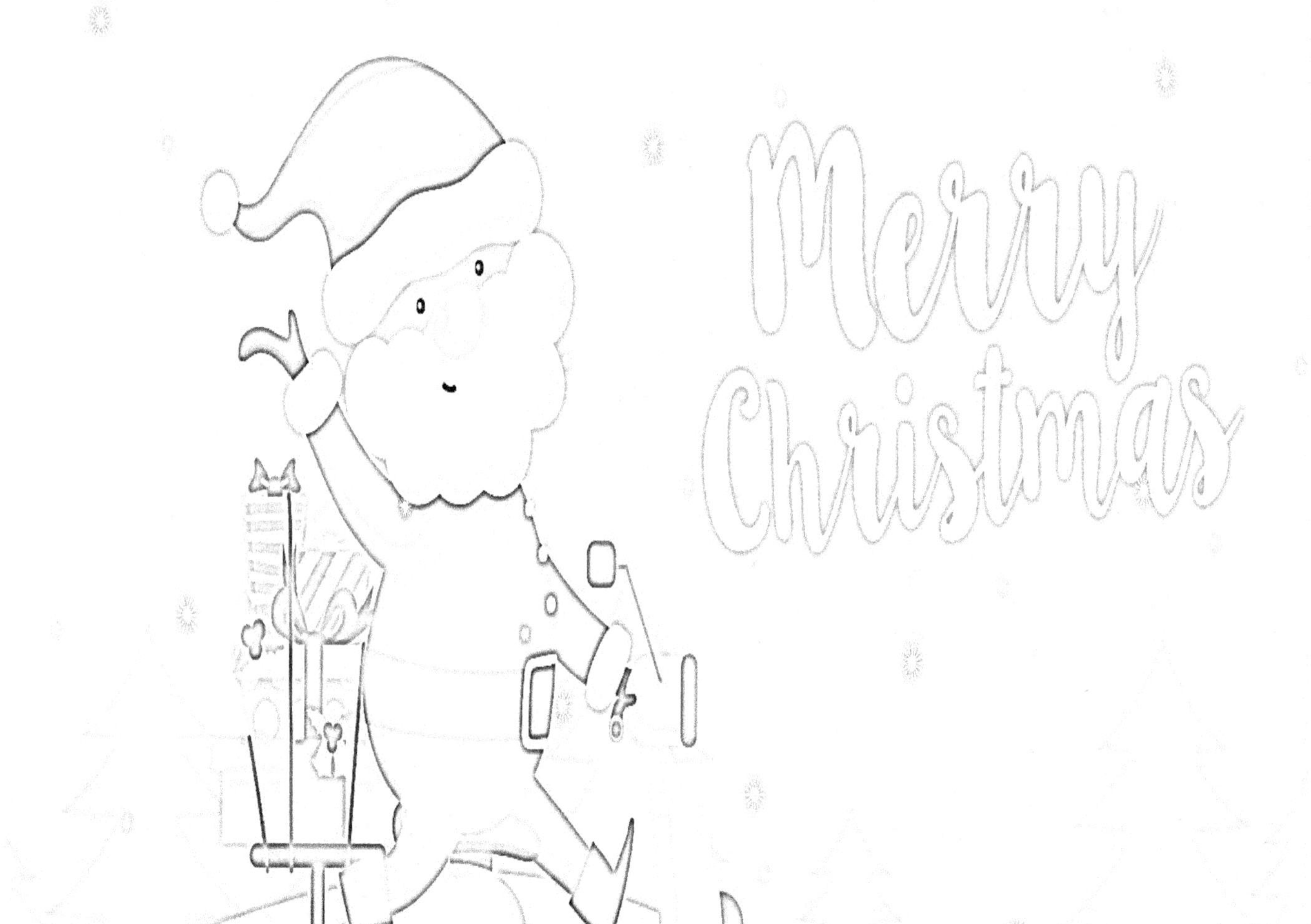
Merry Christmas

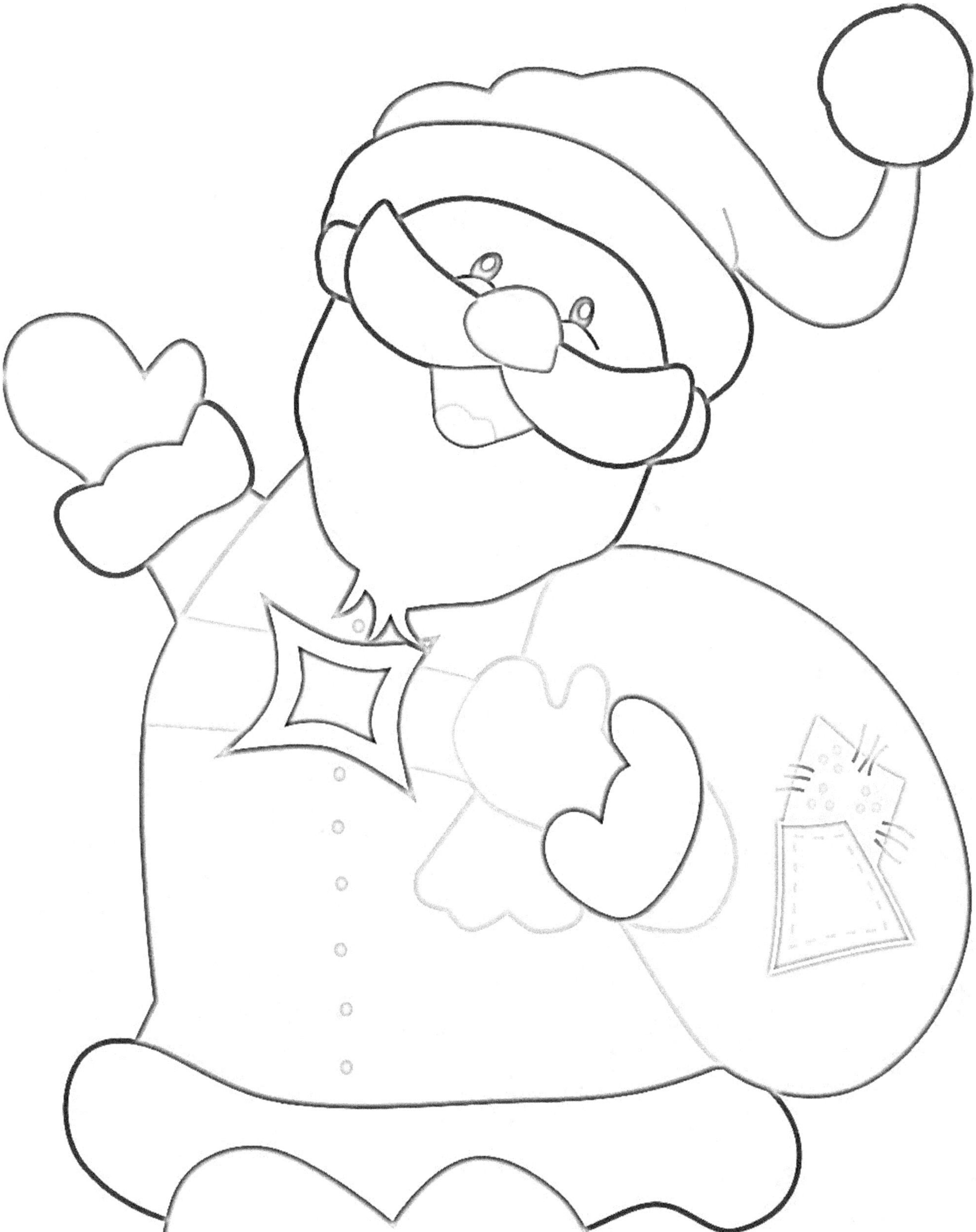

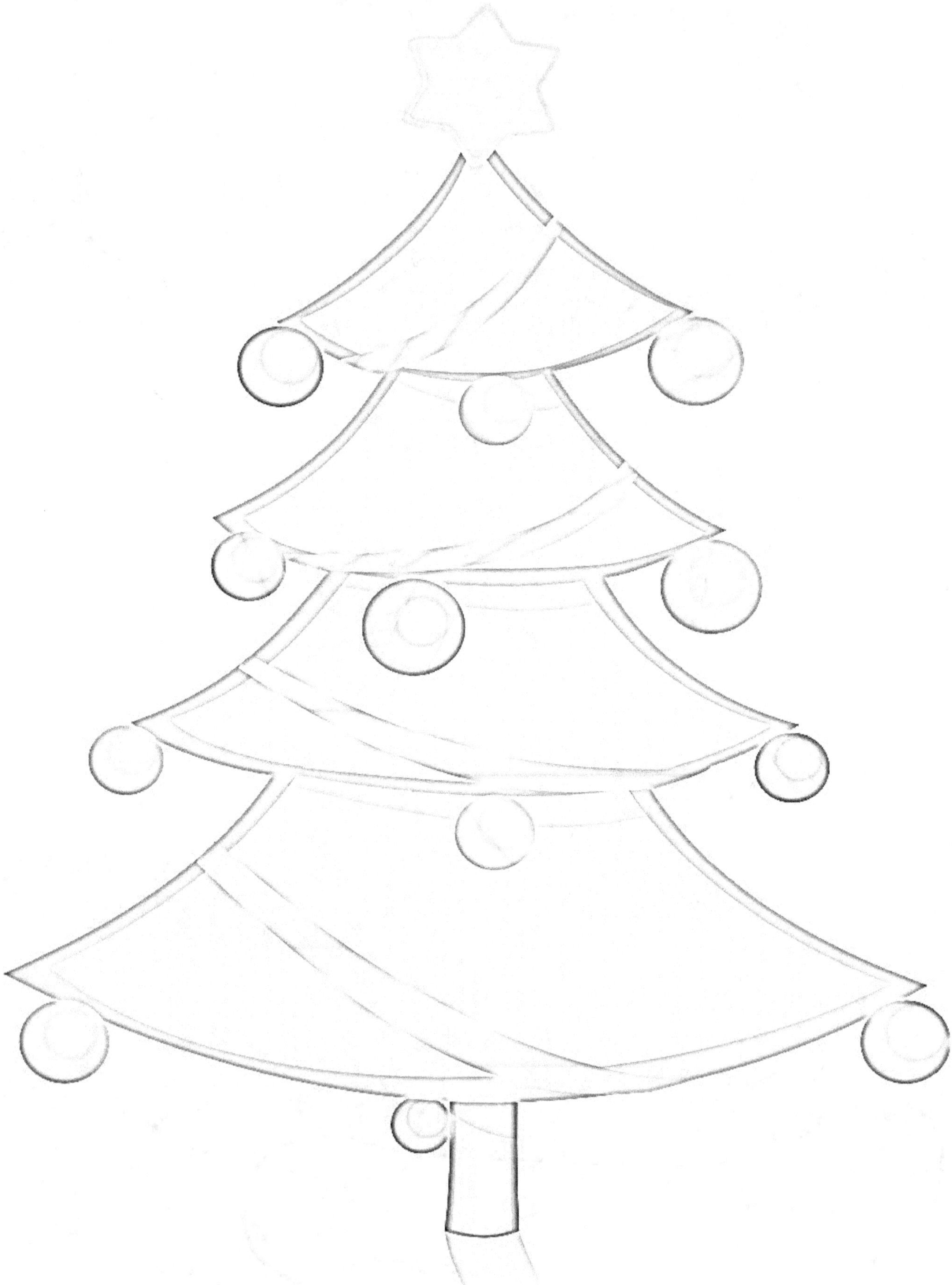

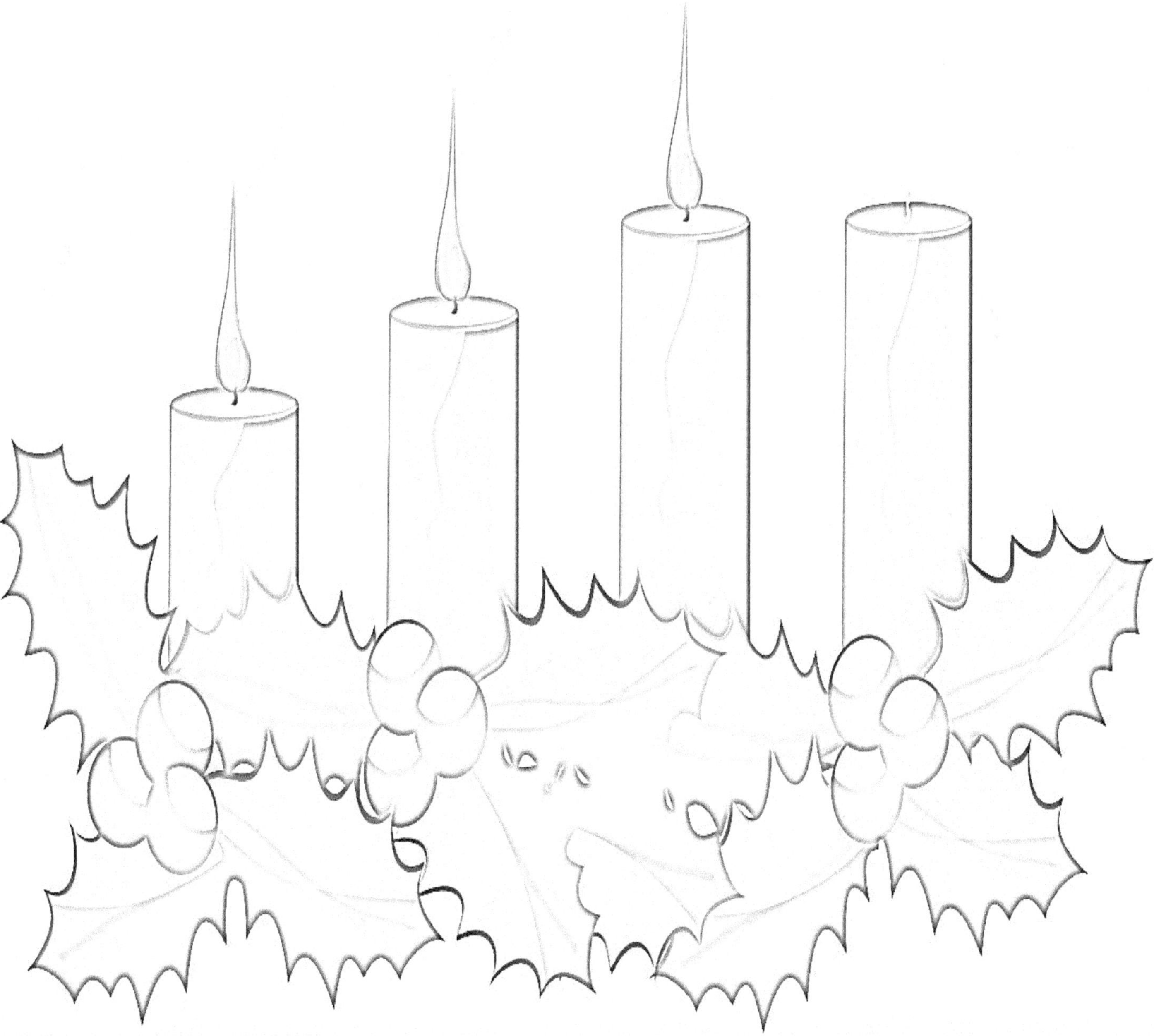

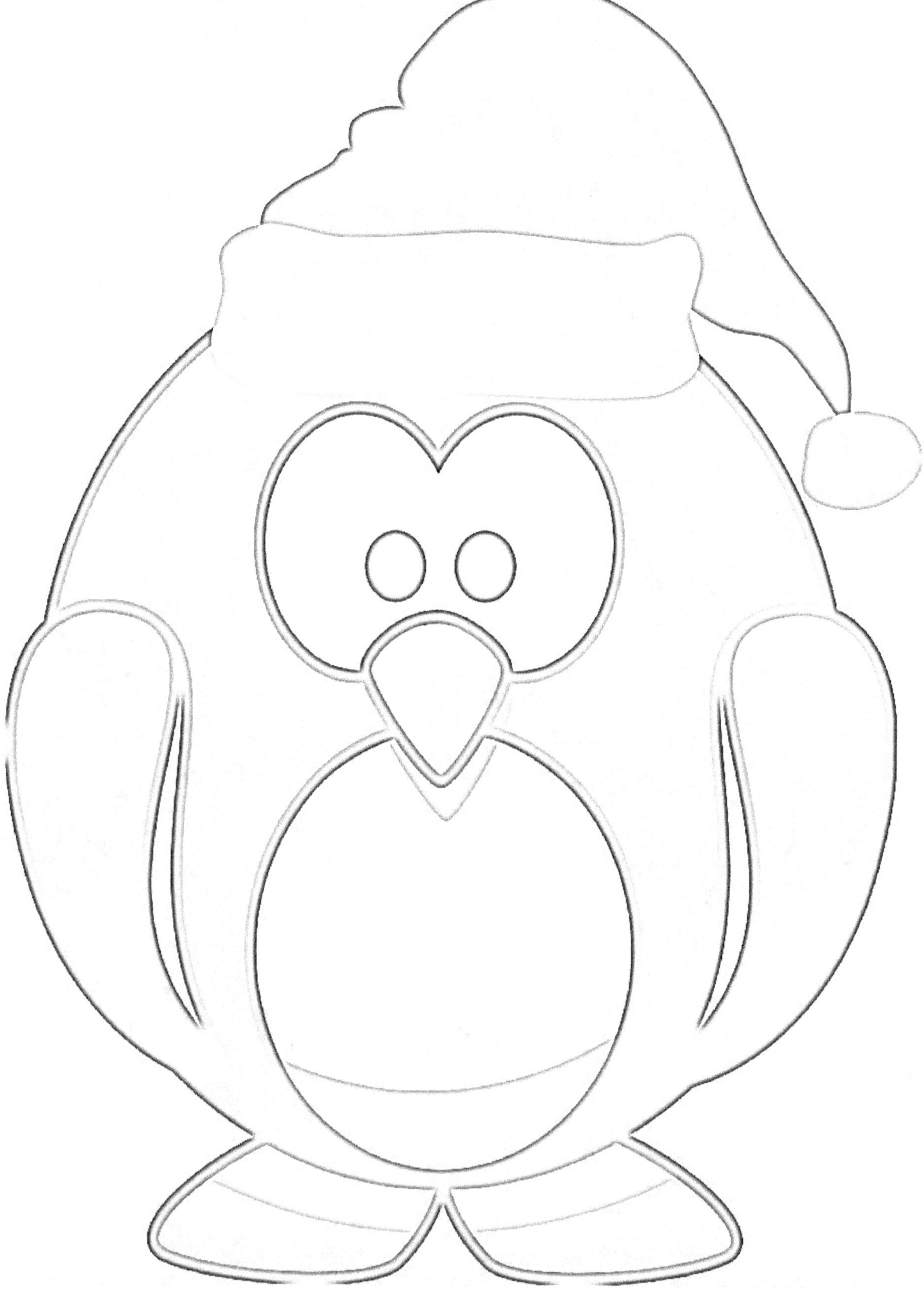

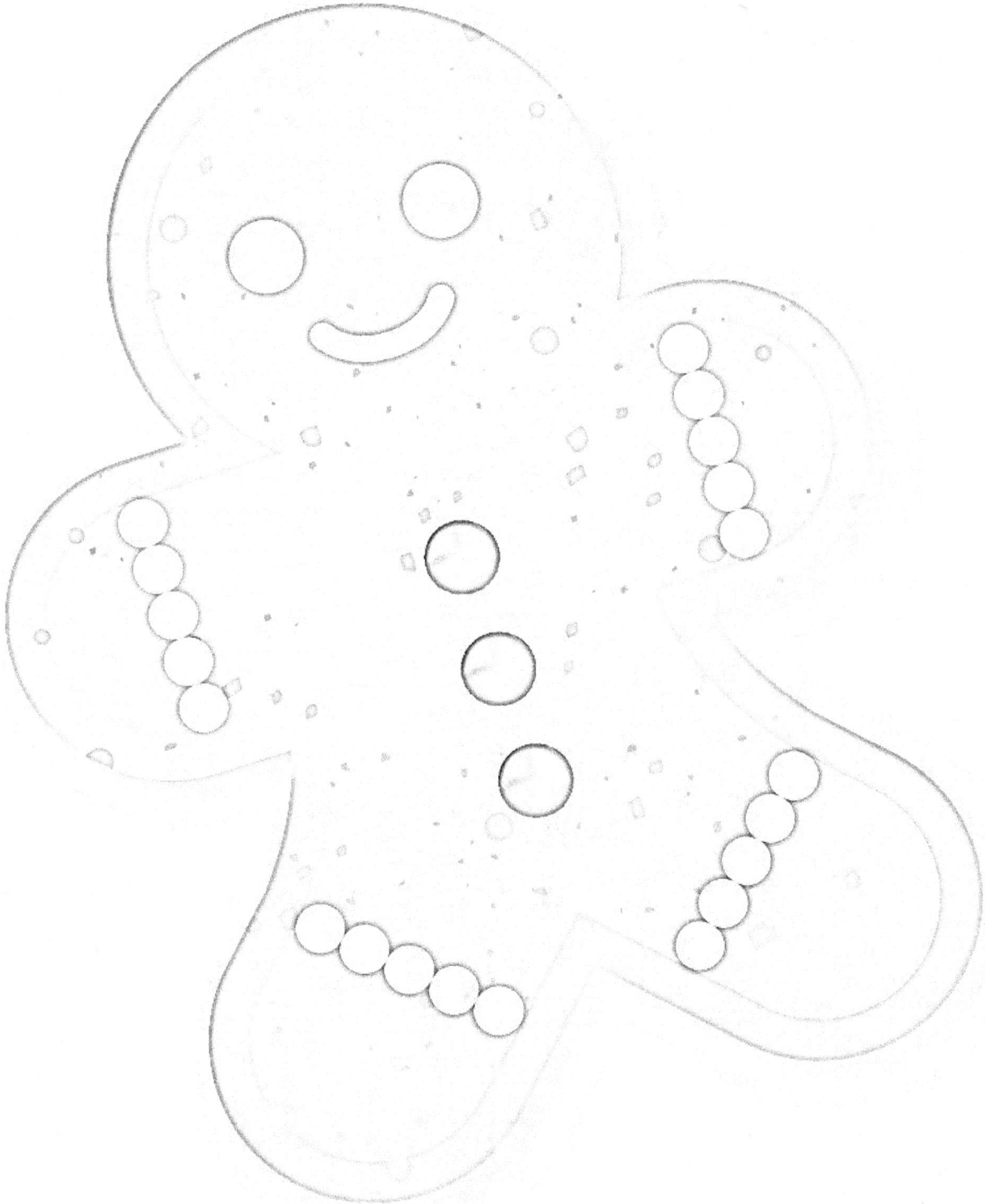

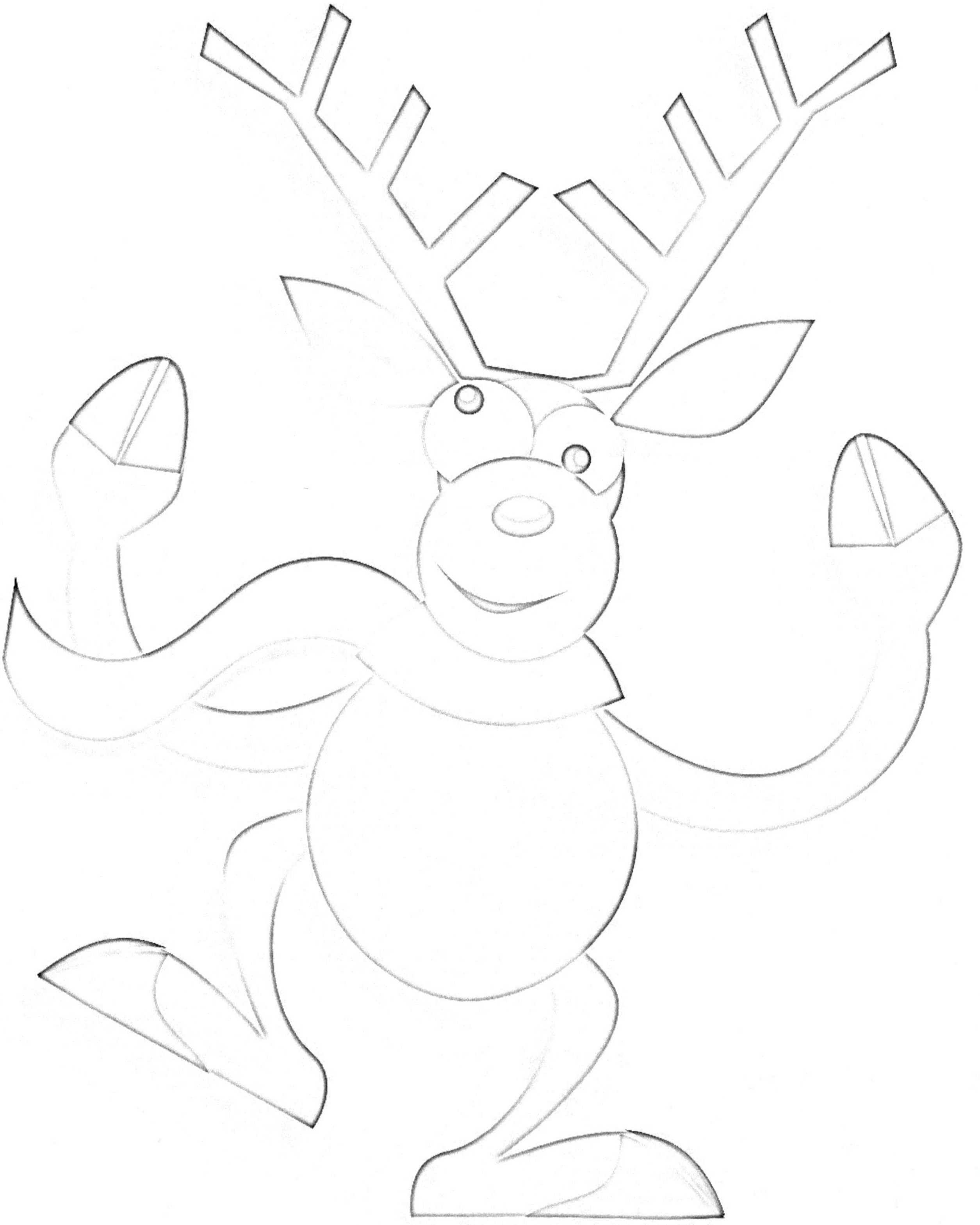

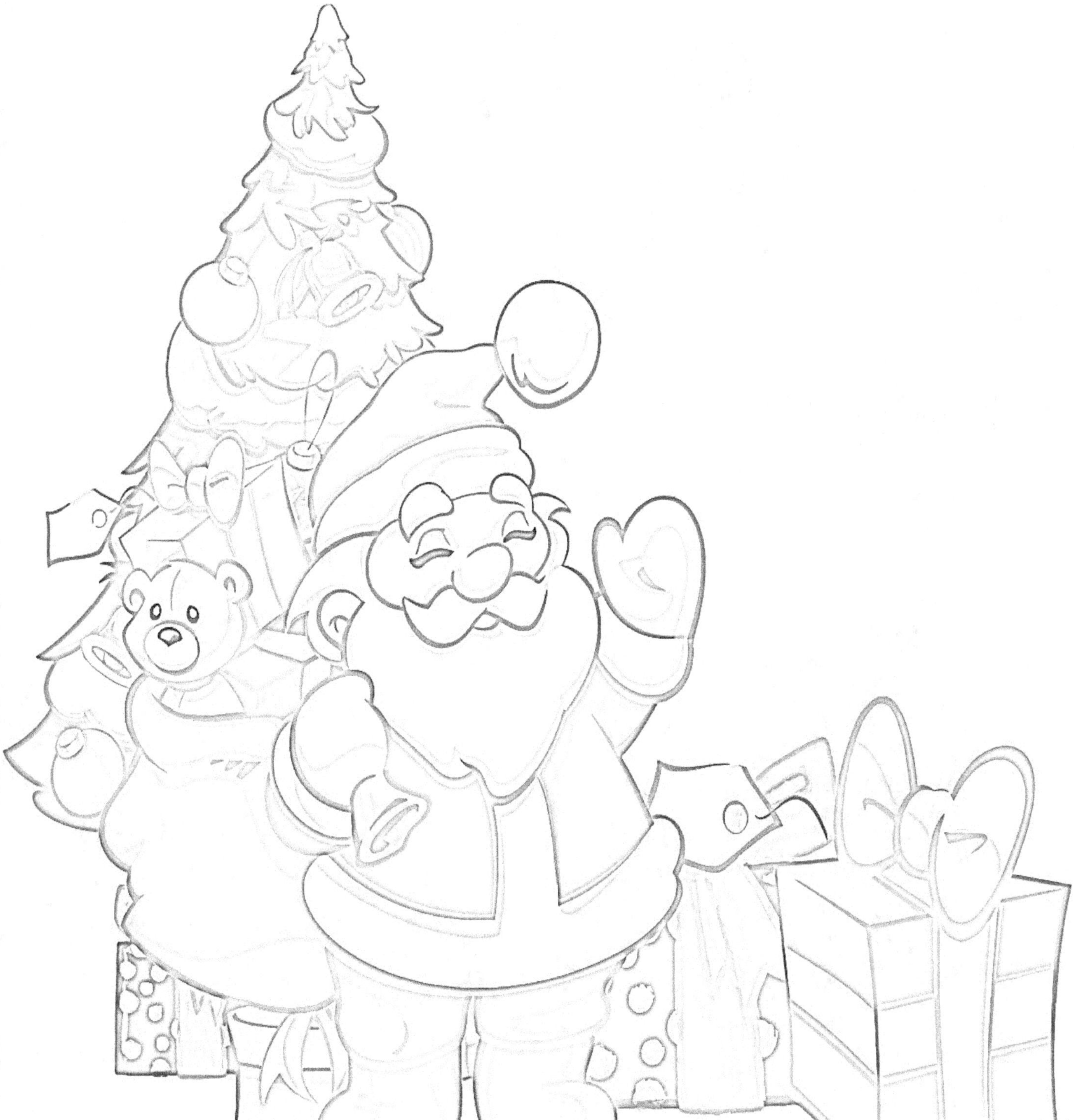

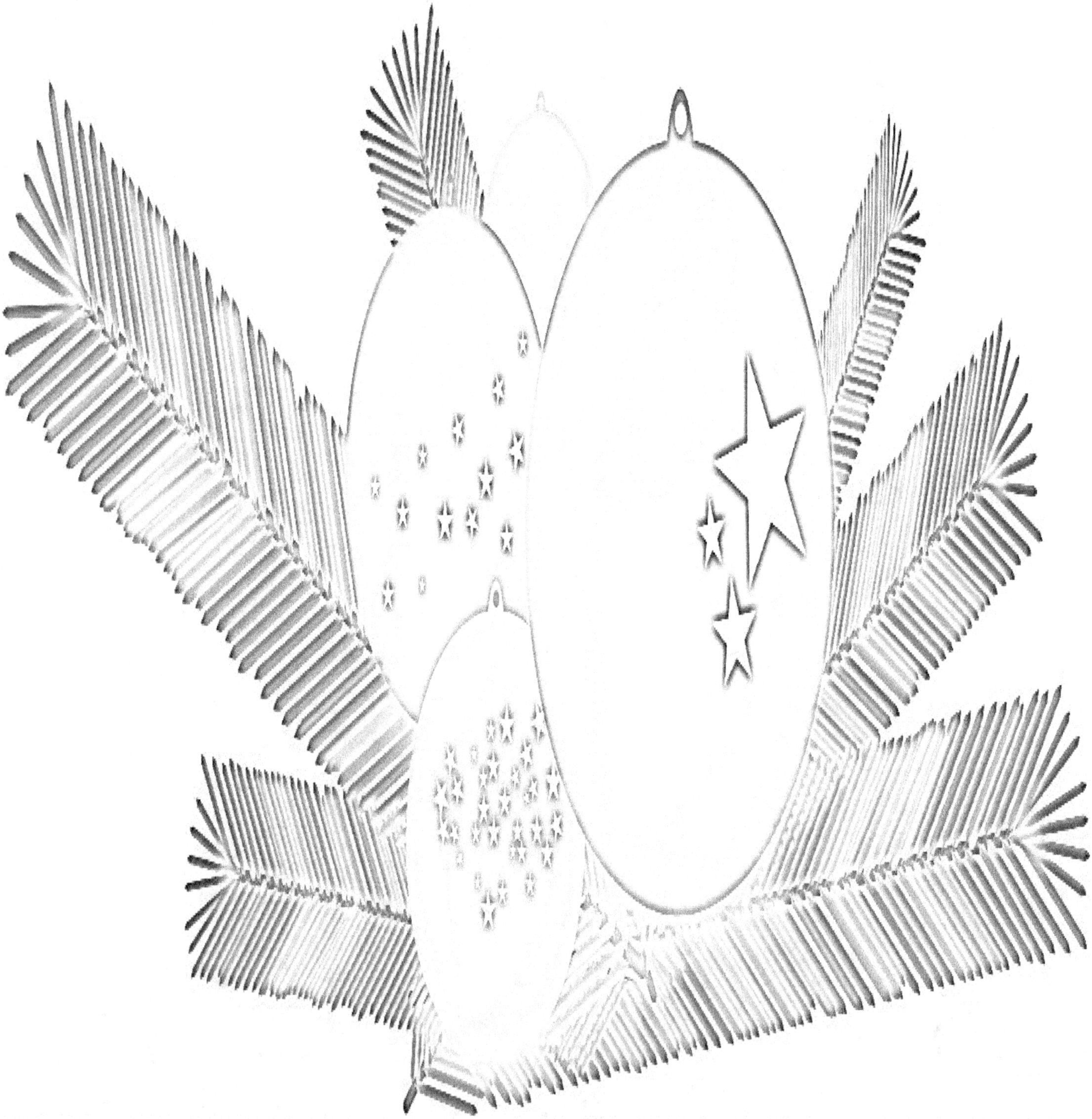

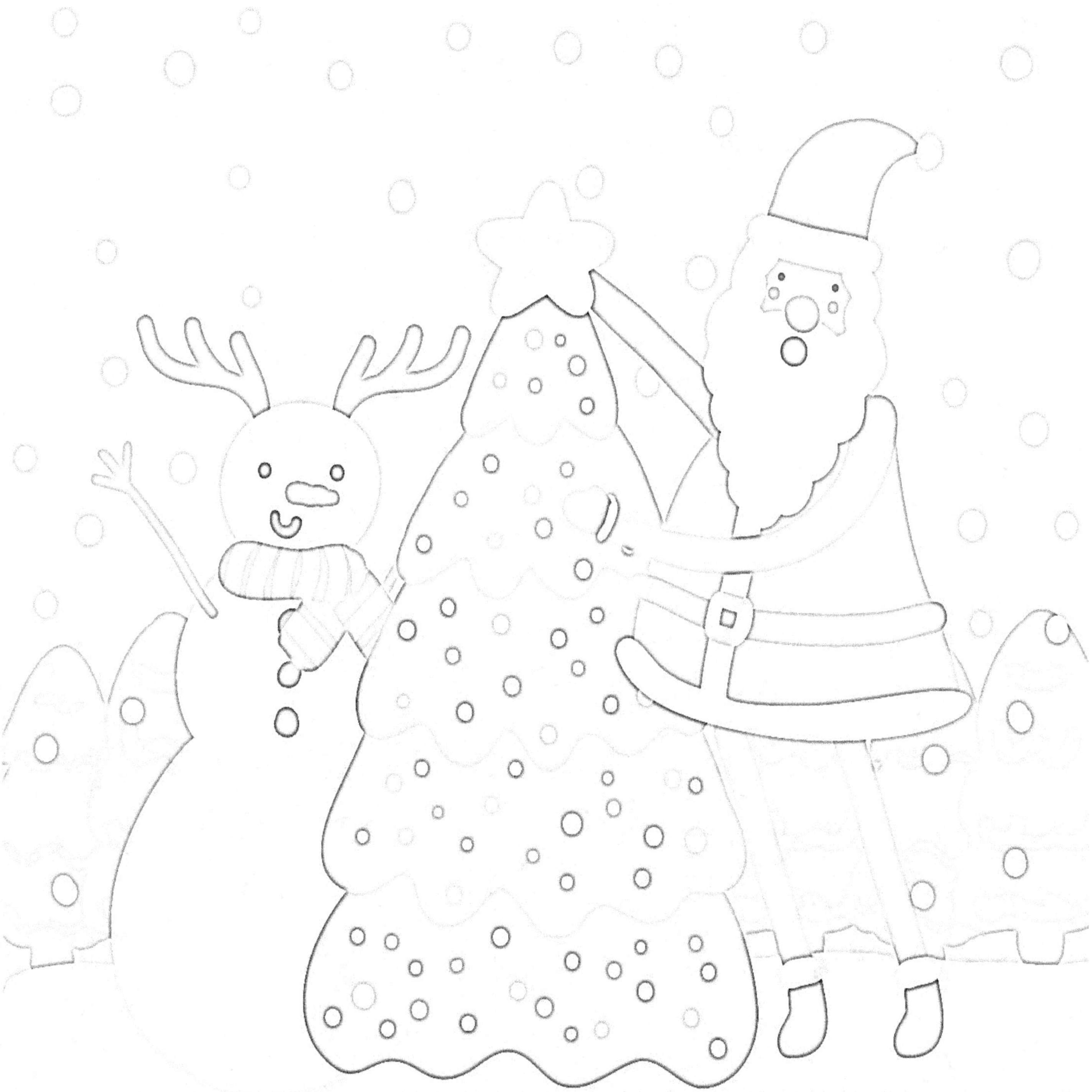

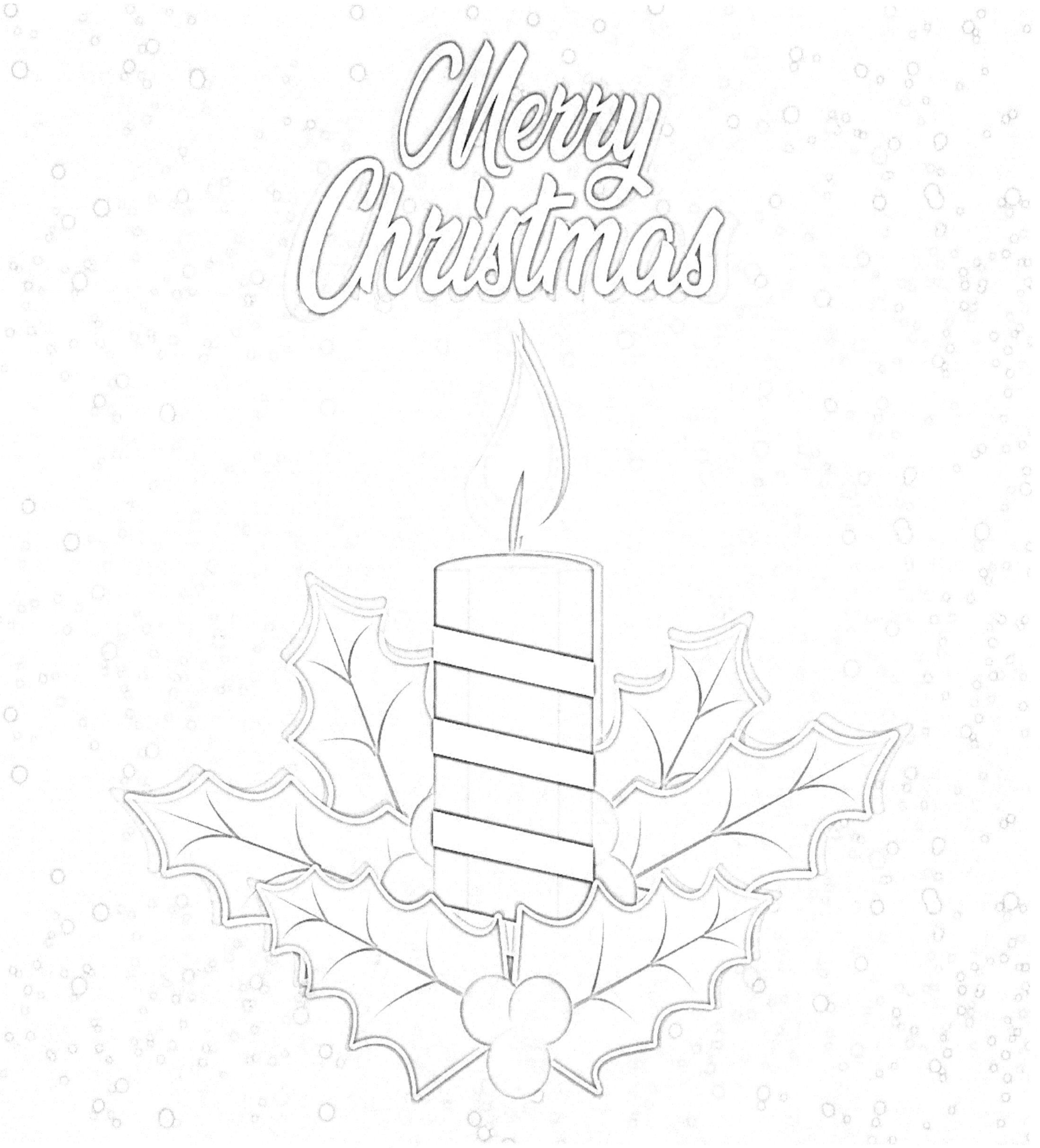
Merry
Christmas

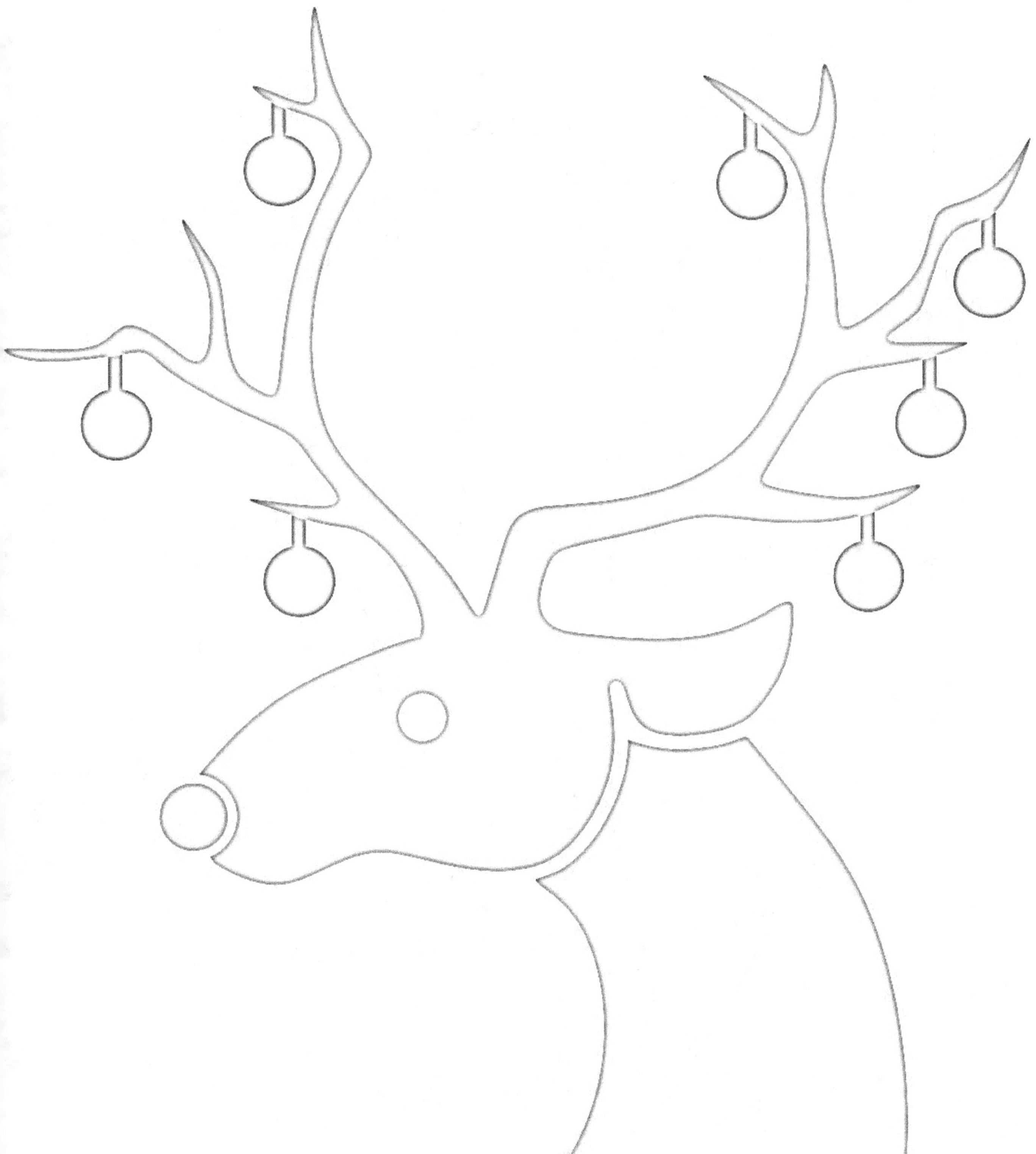

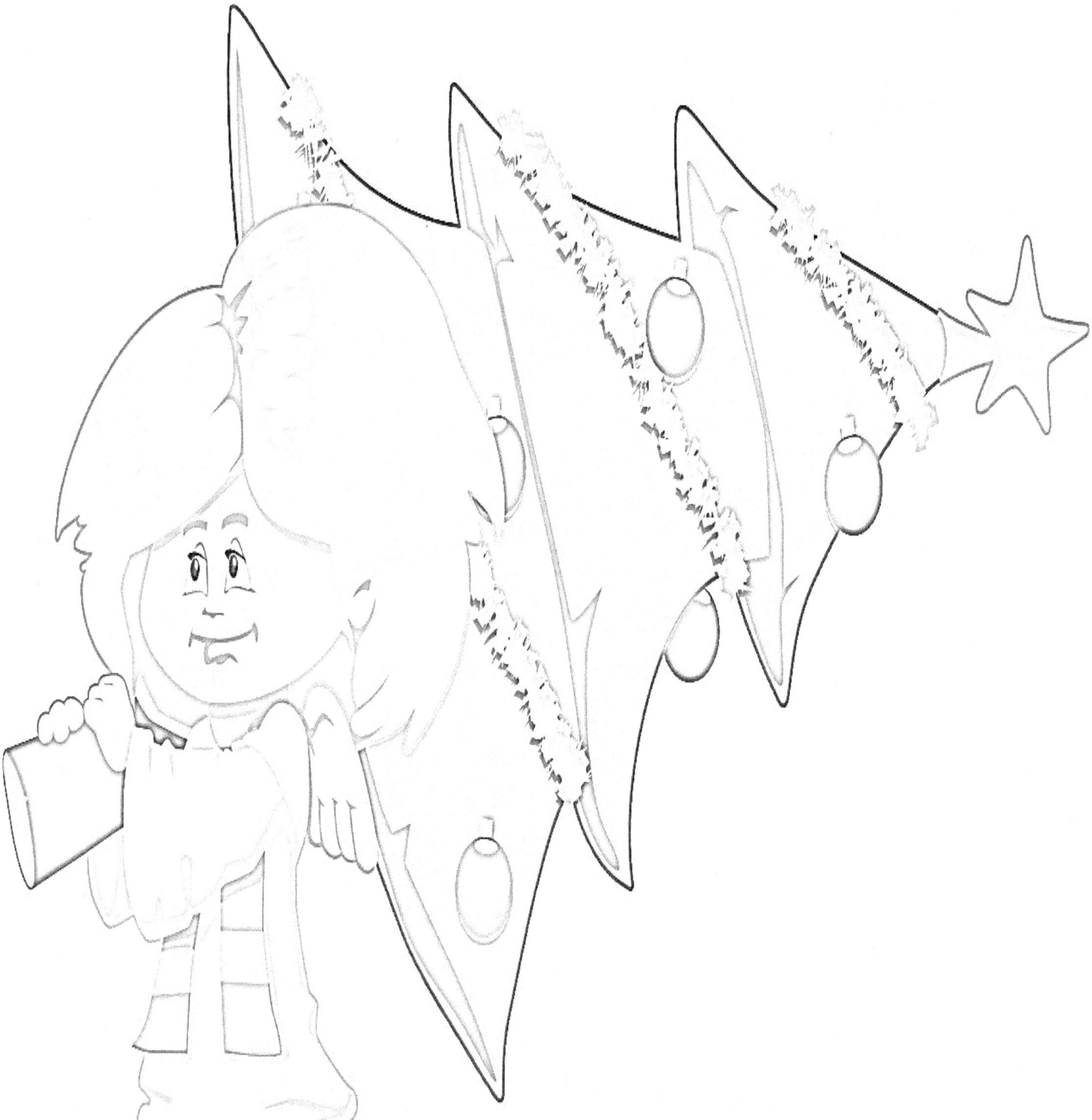

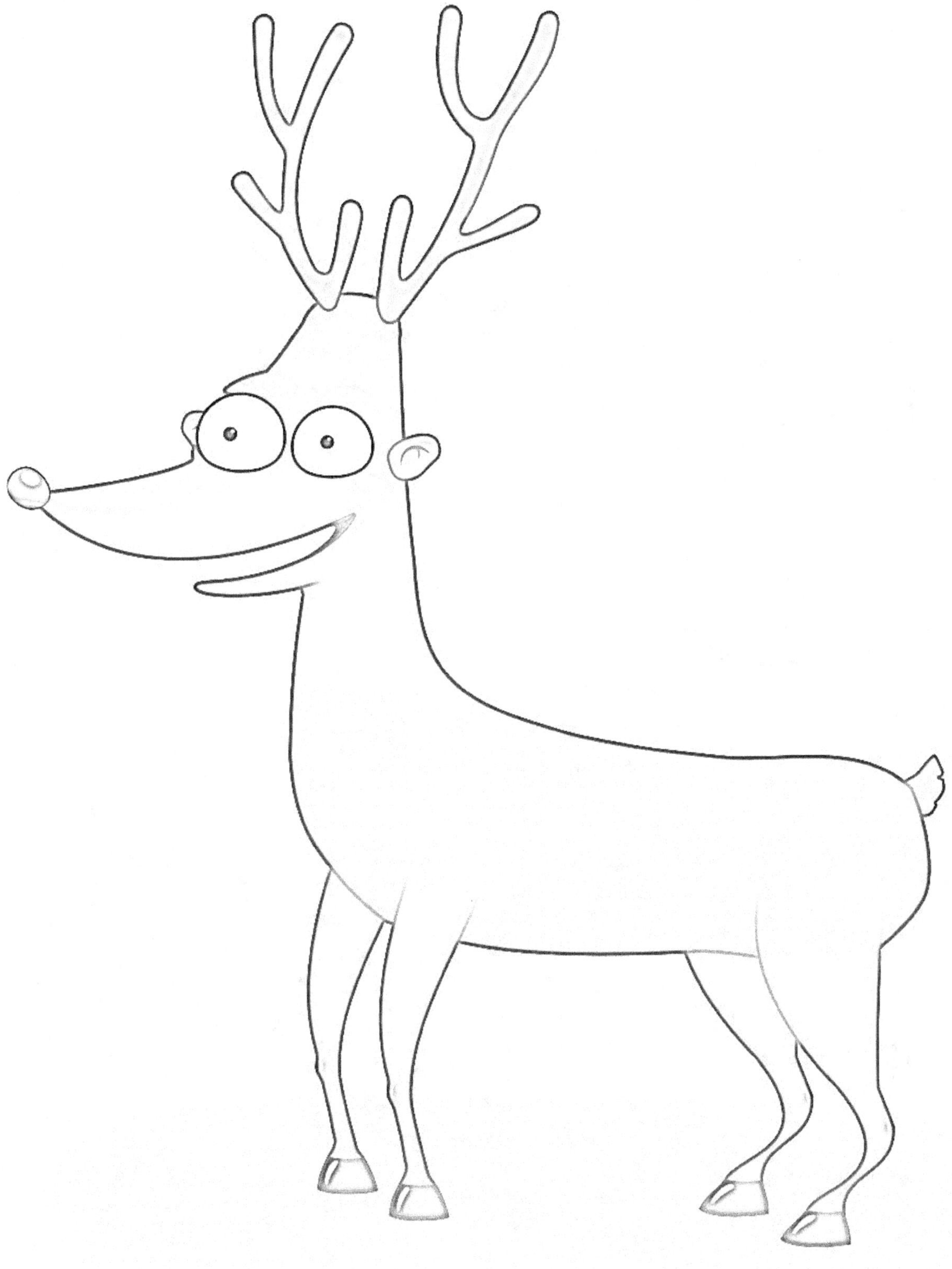

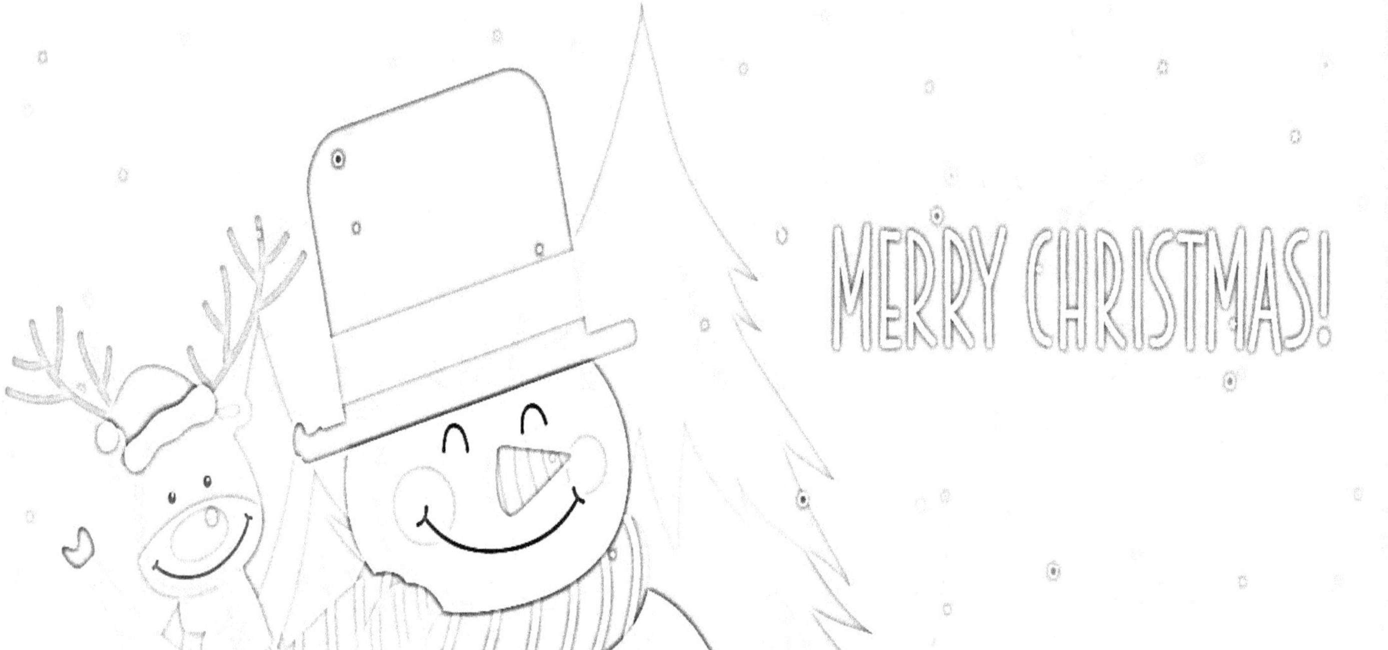
MERRY CHRISTMAS!

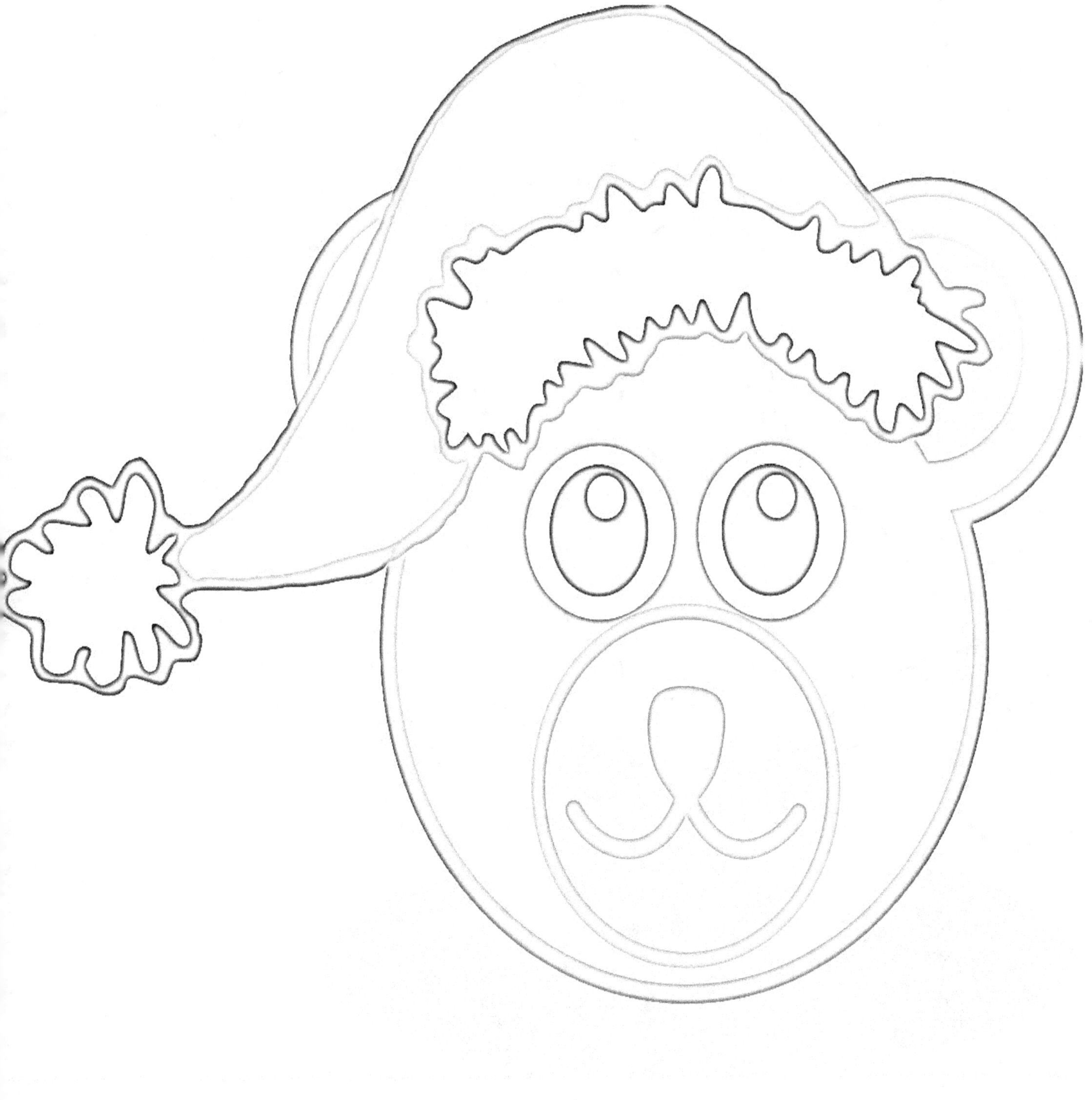

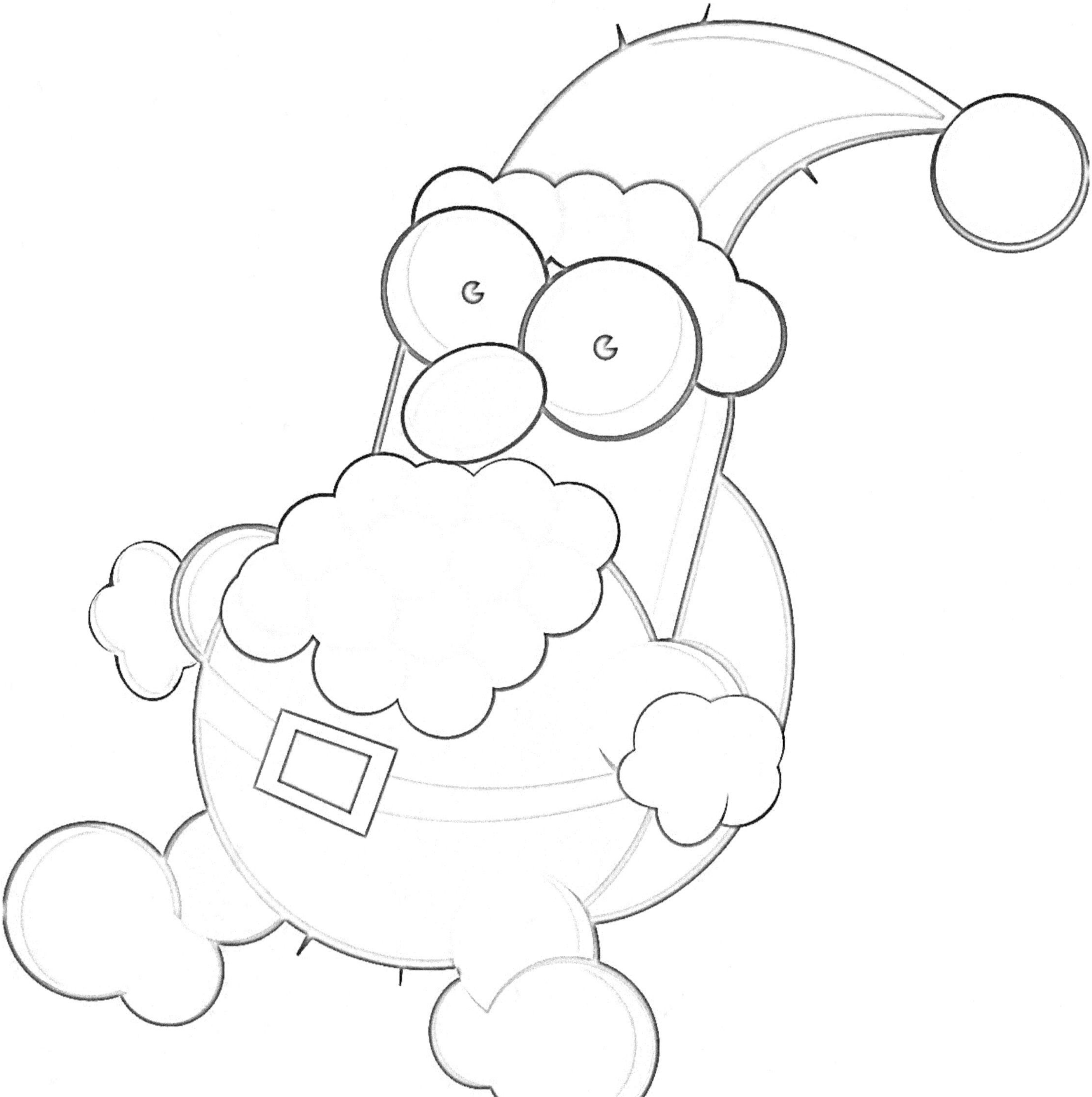

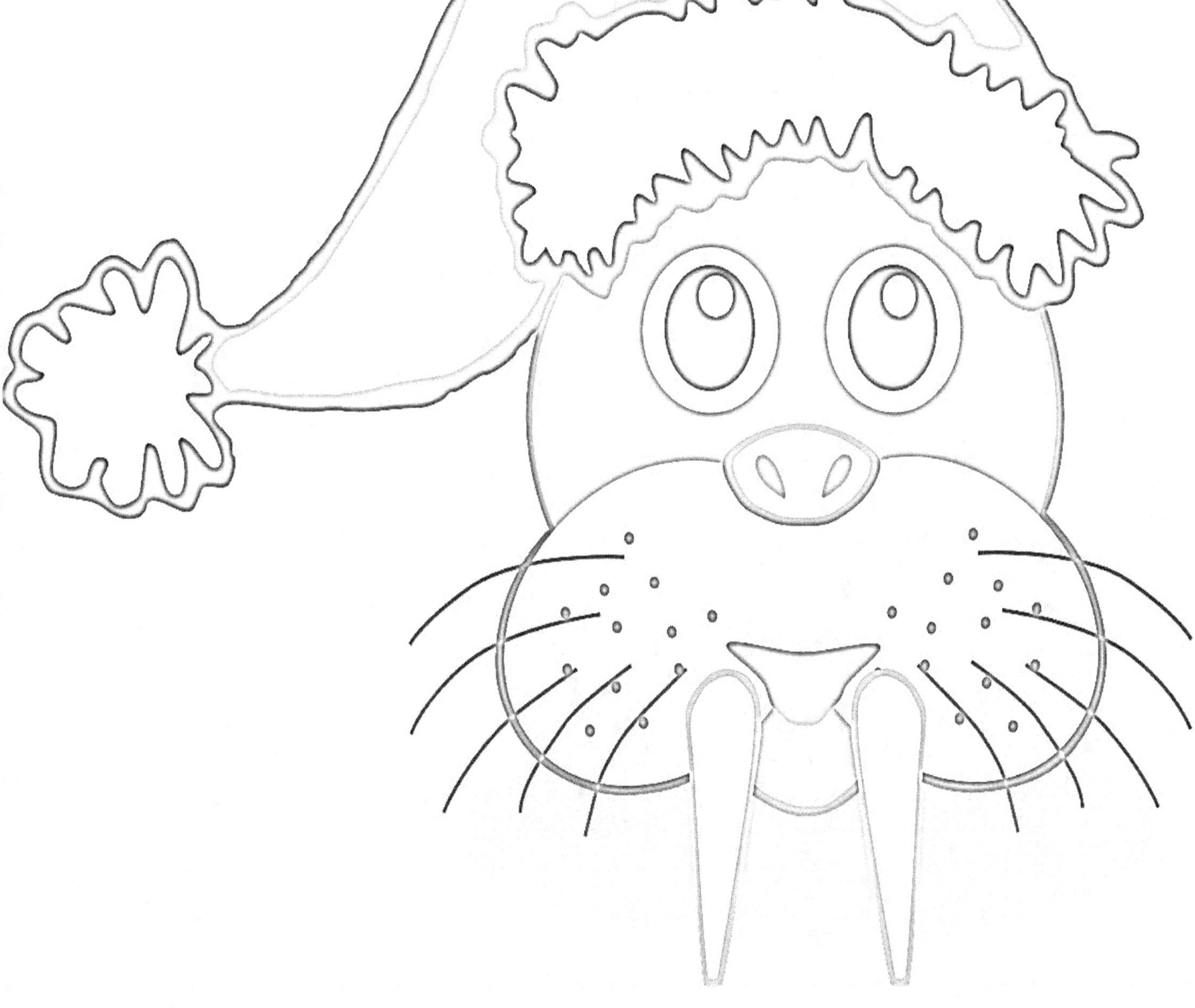

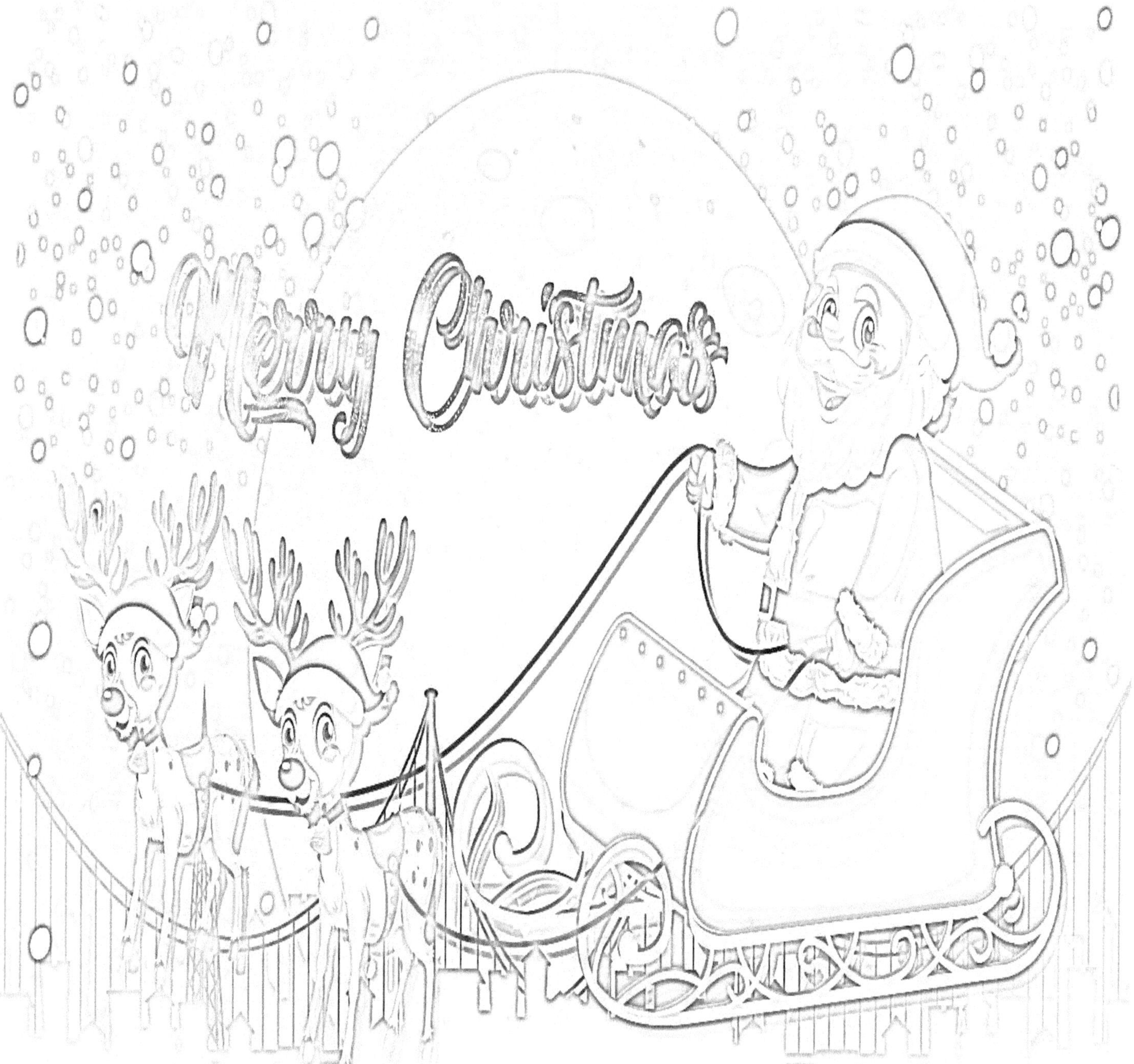
Merry Christmas

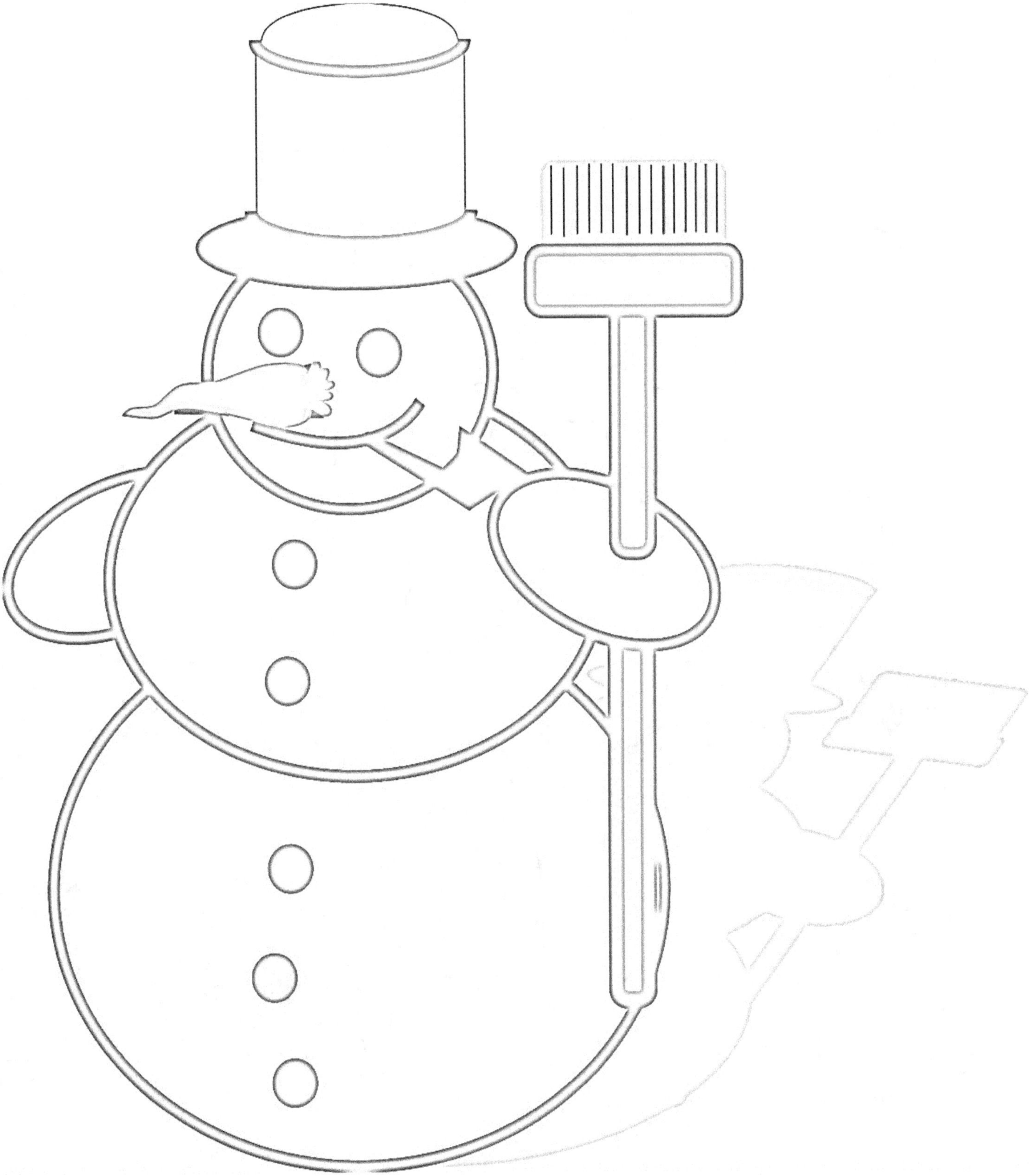

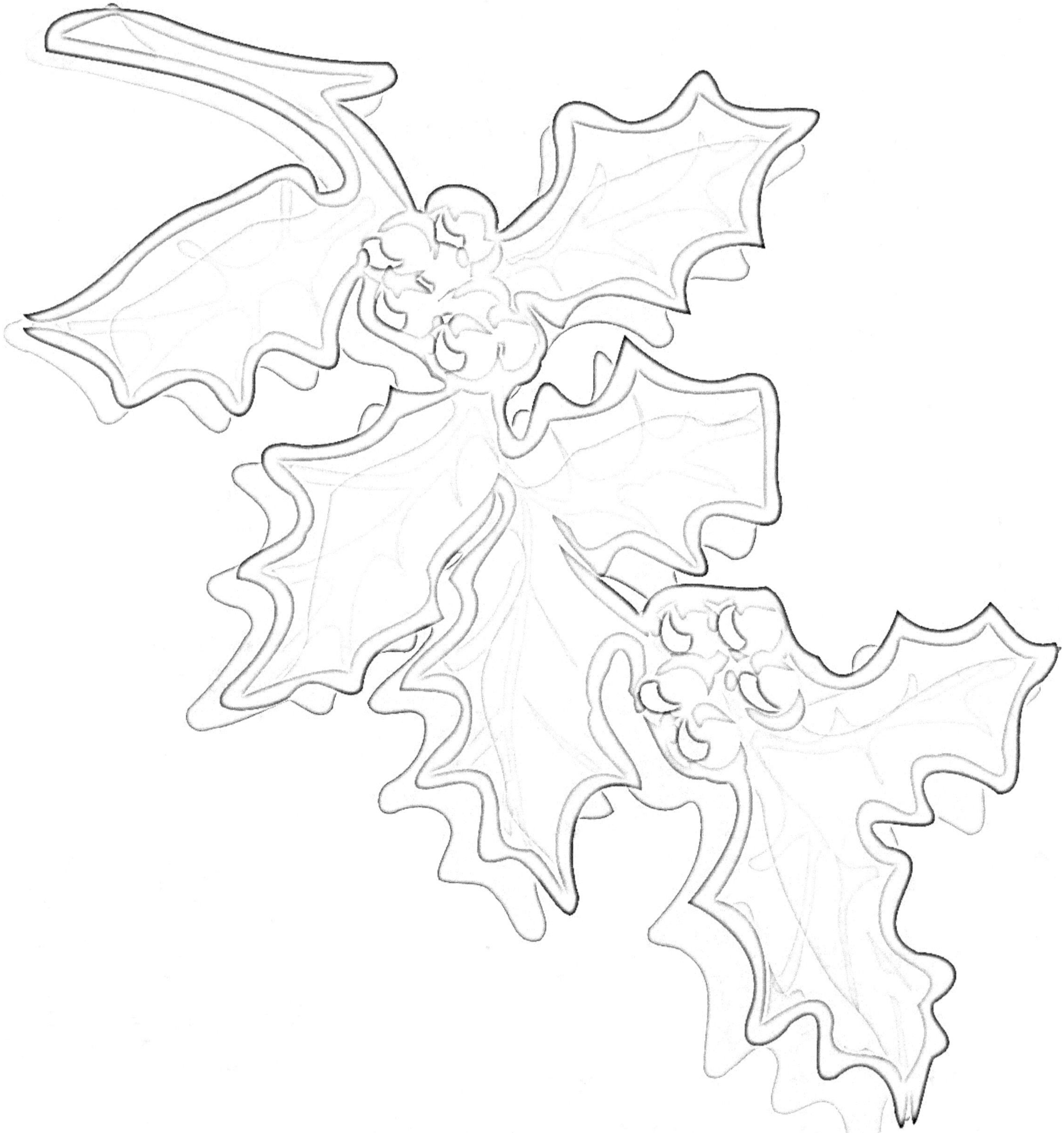

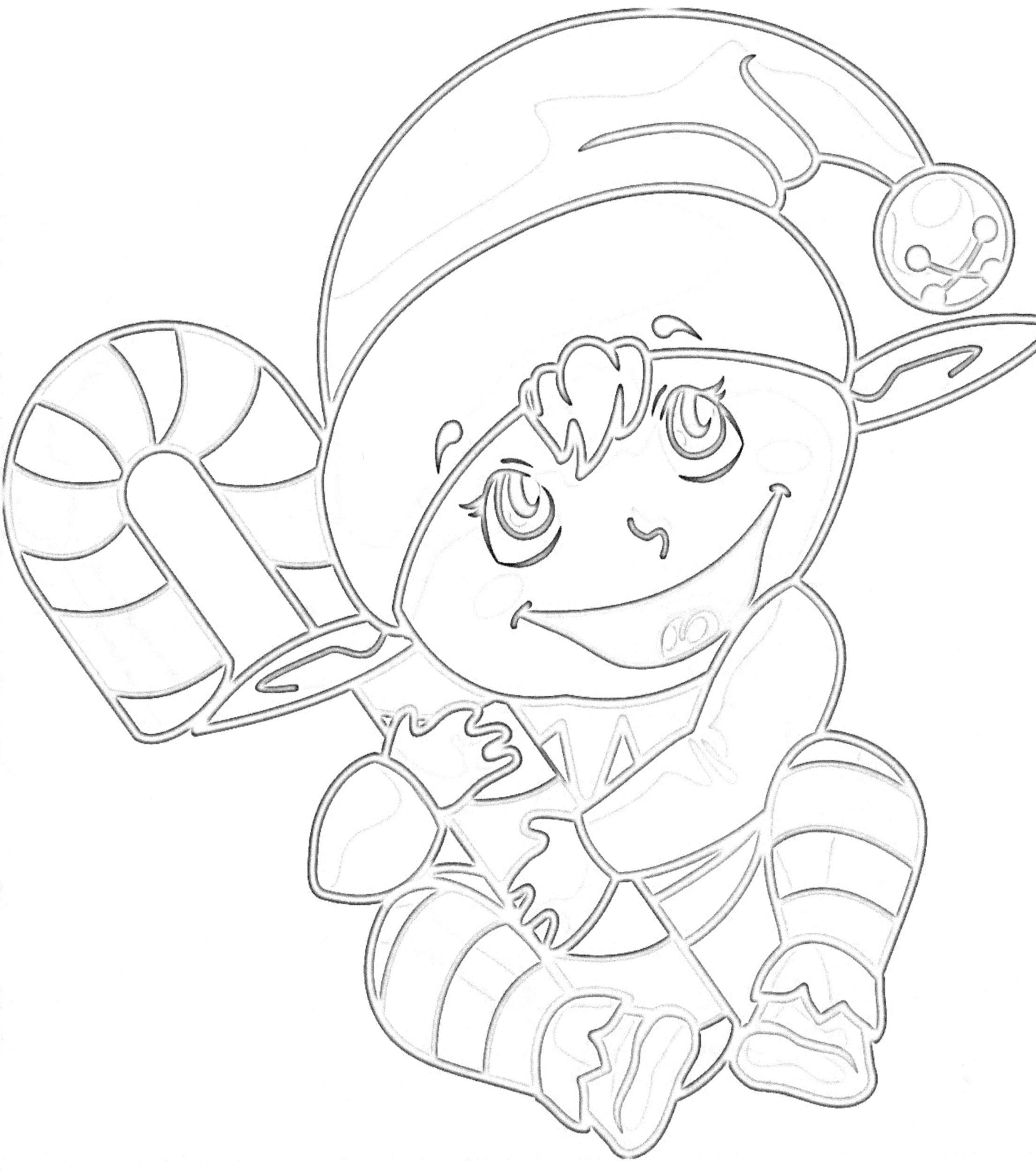

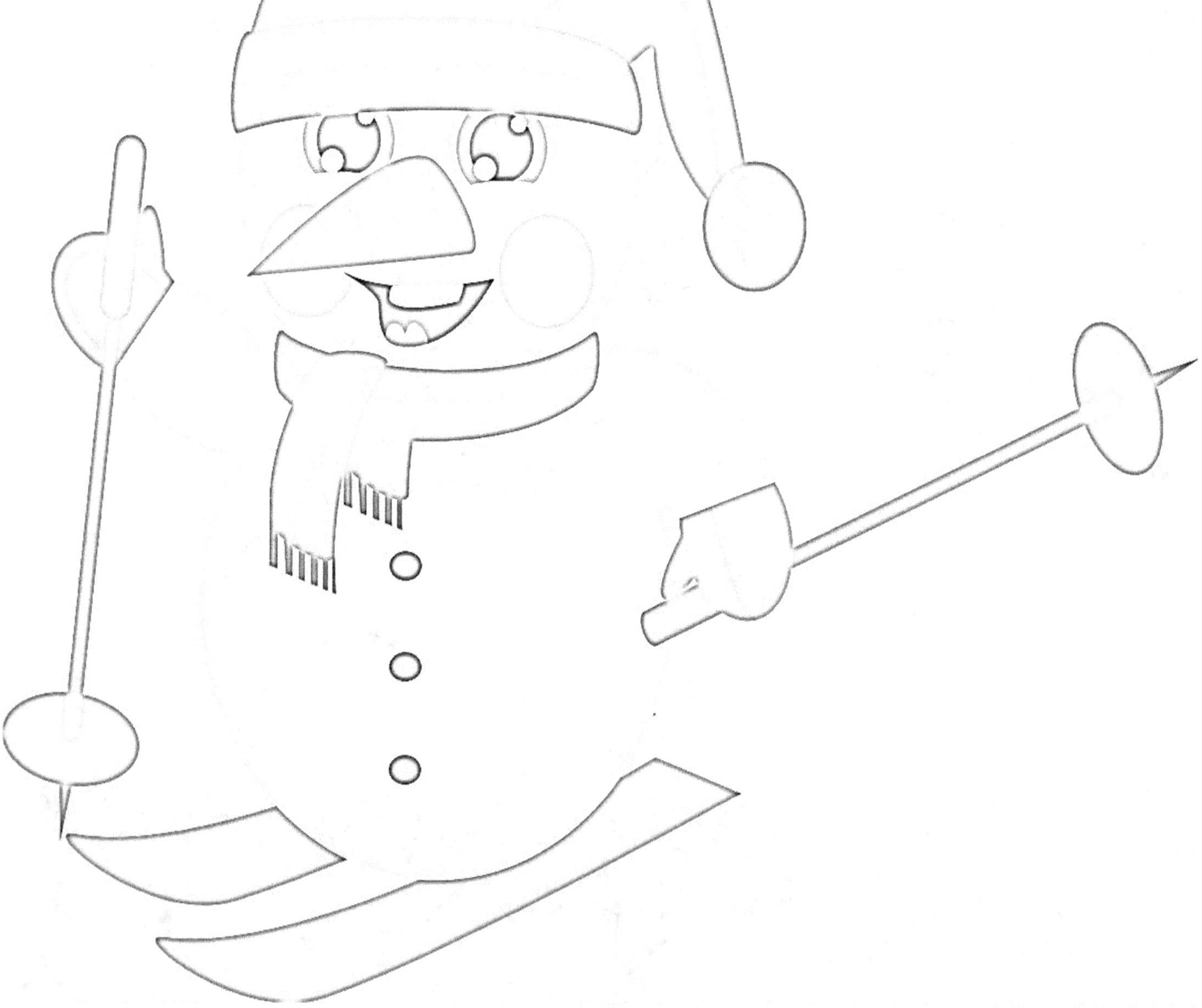

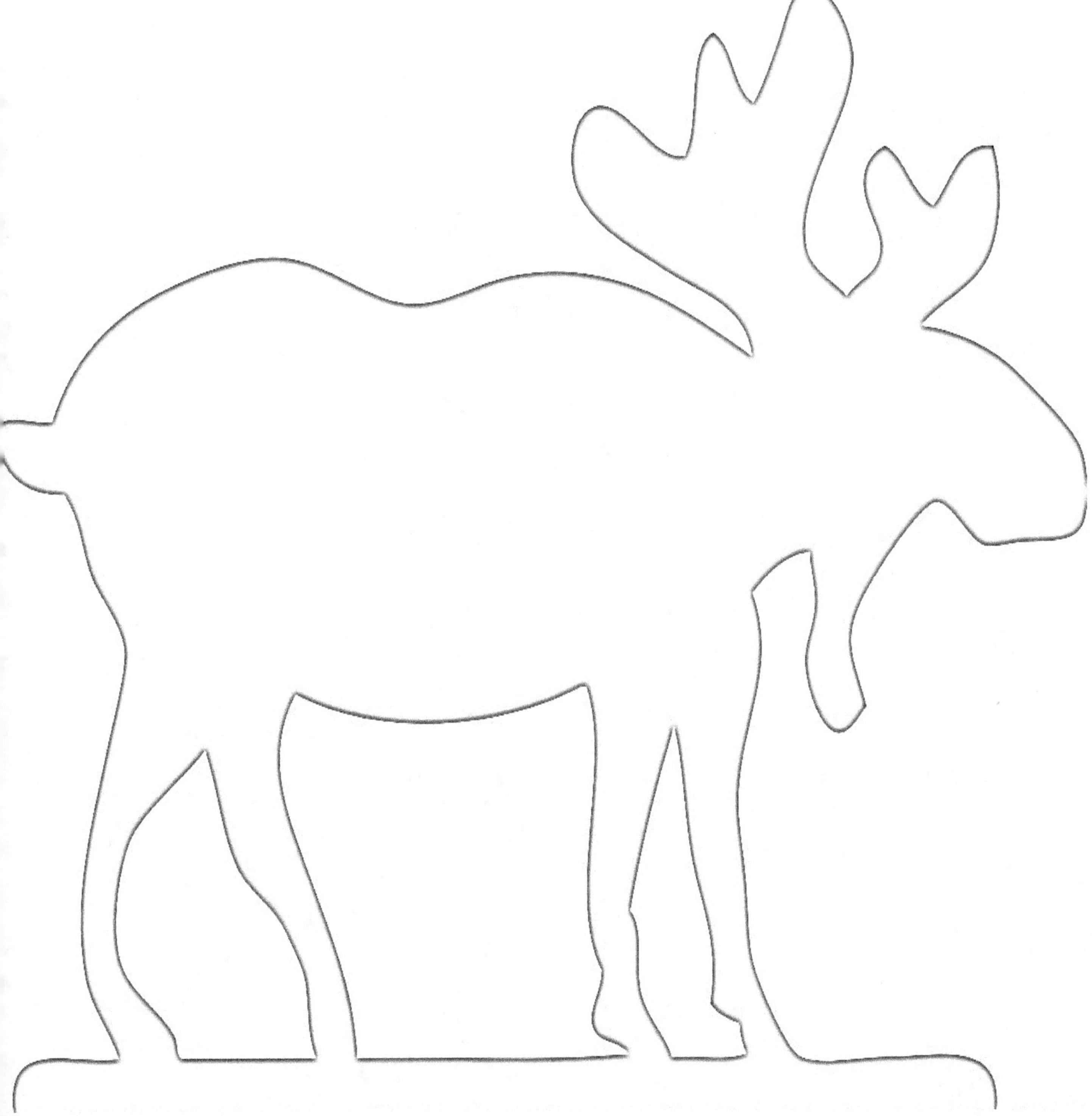

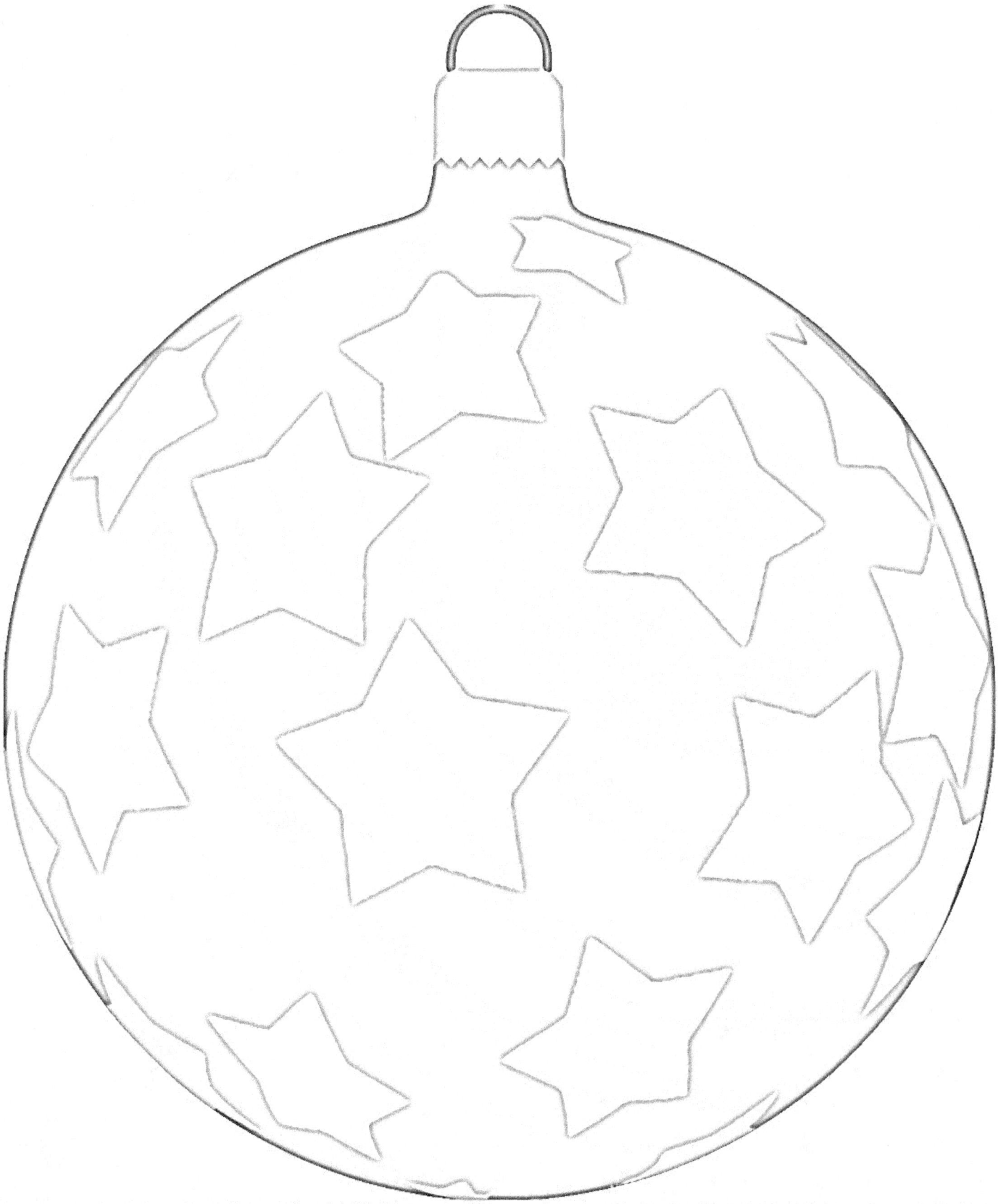

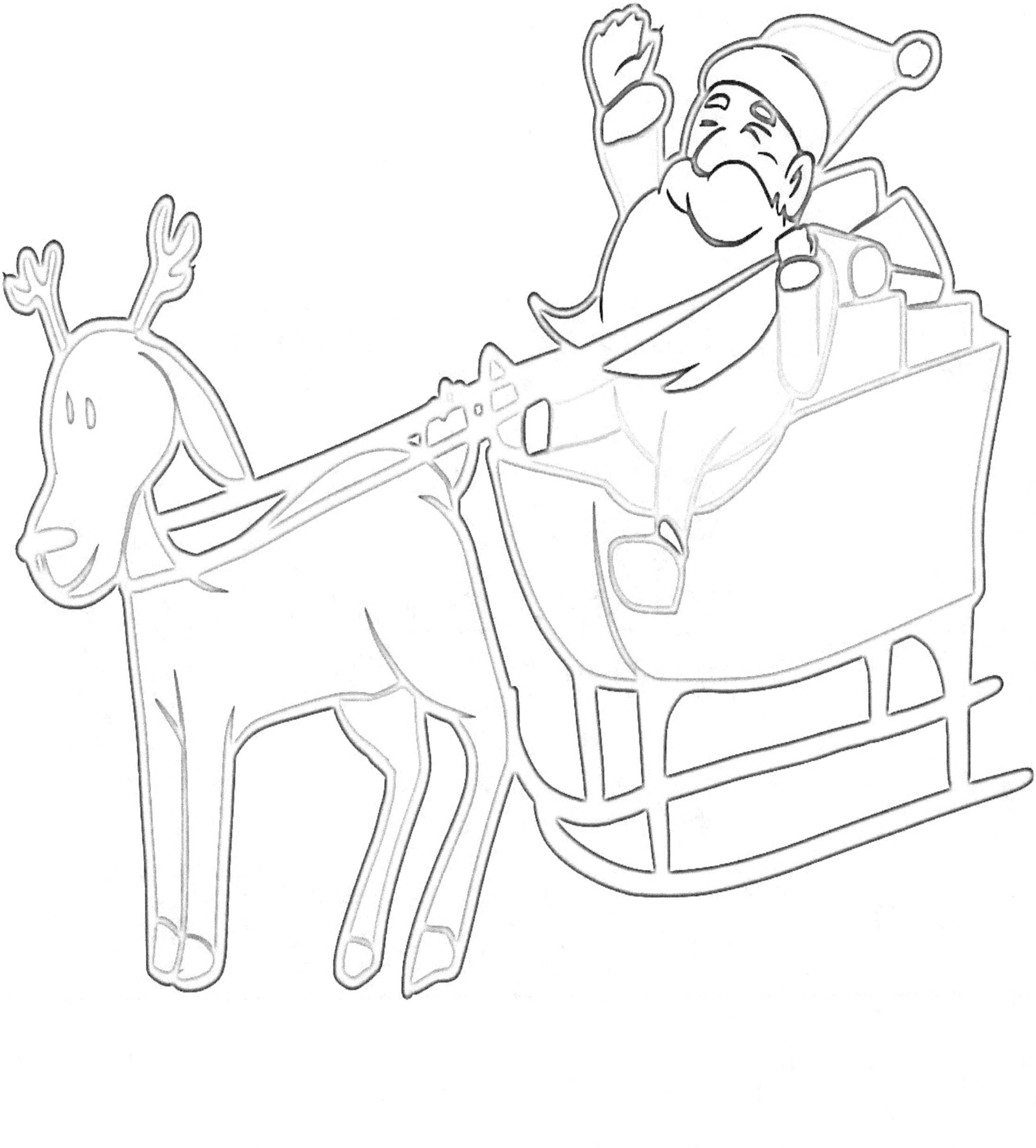

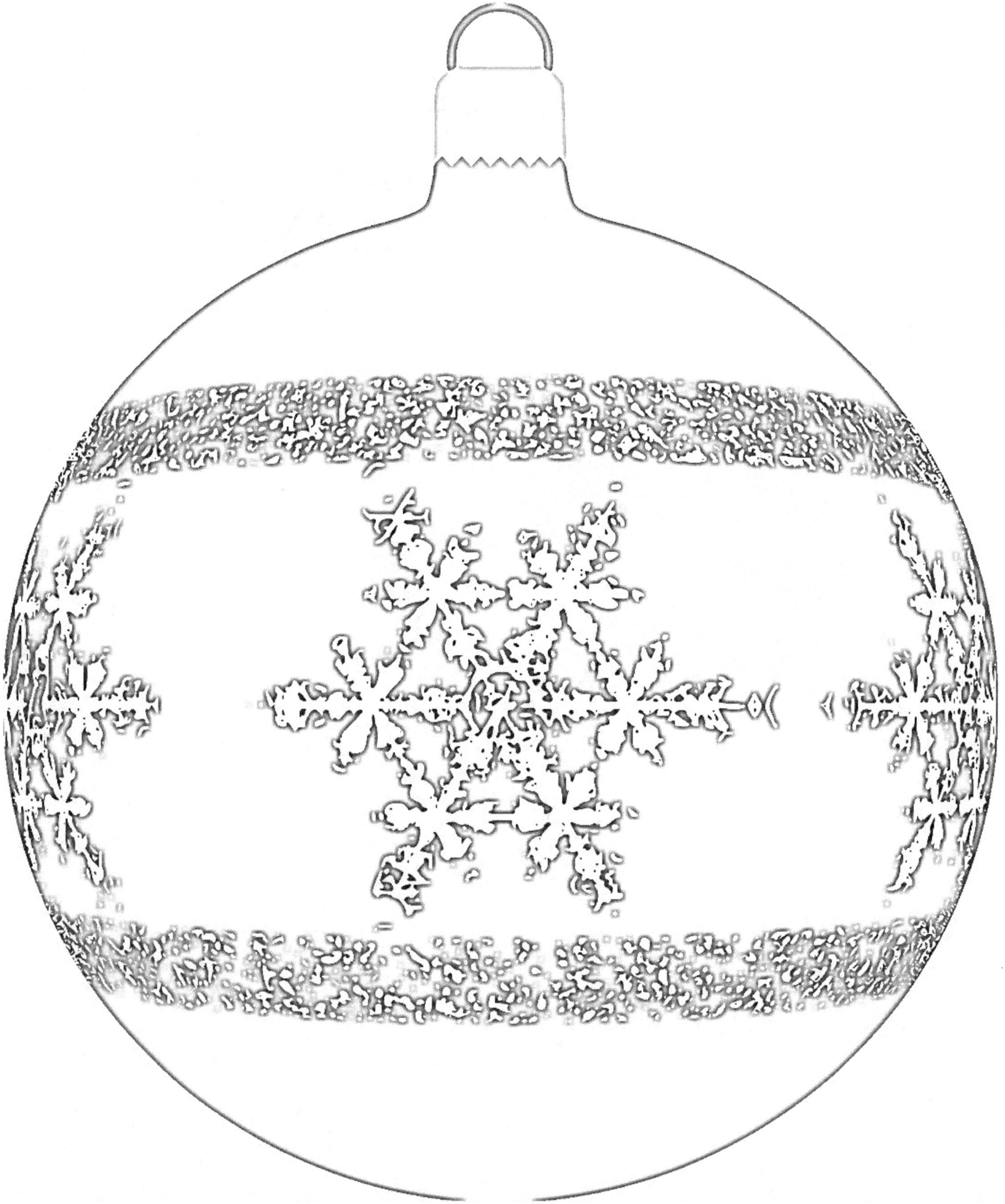

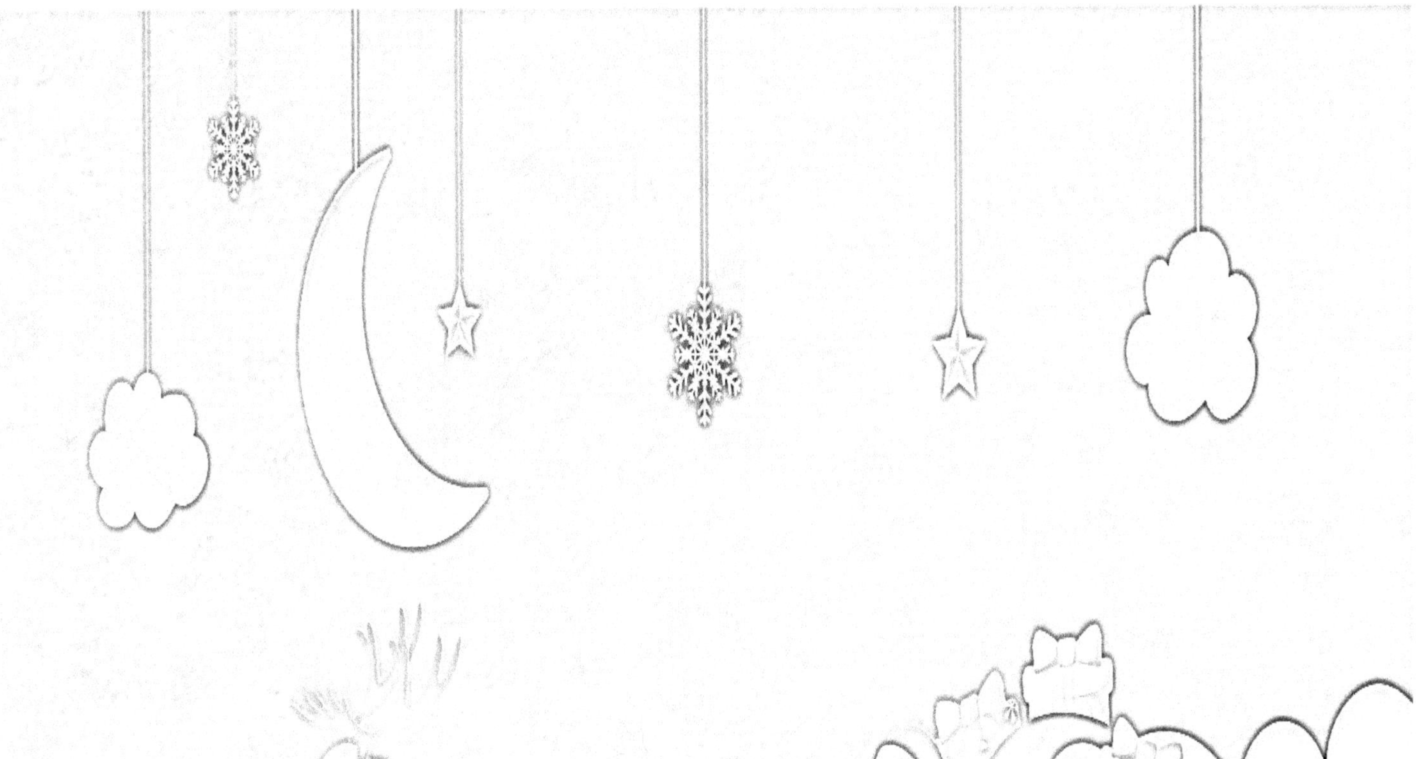

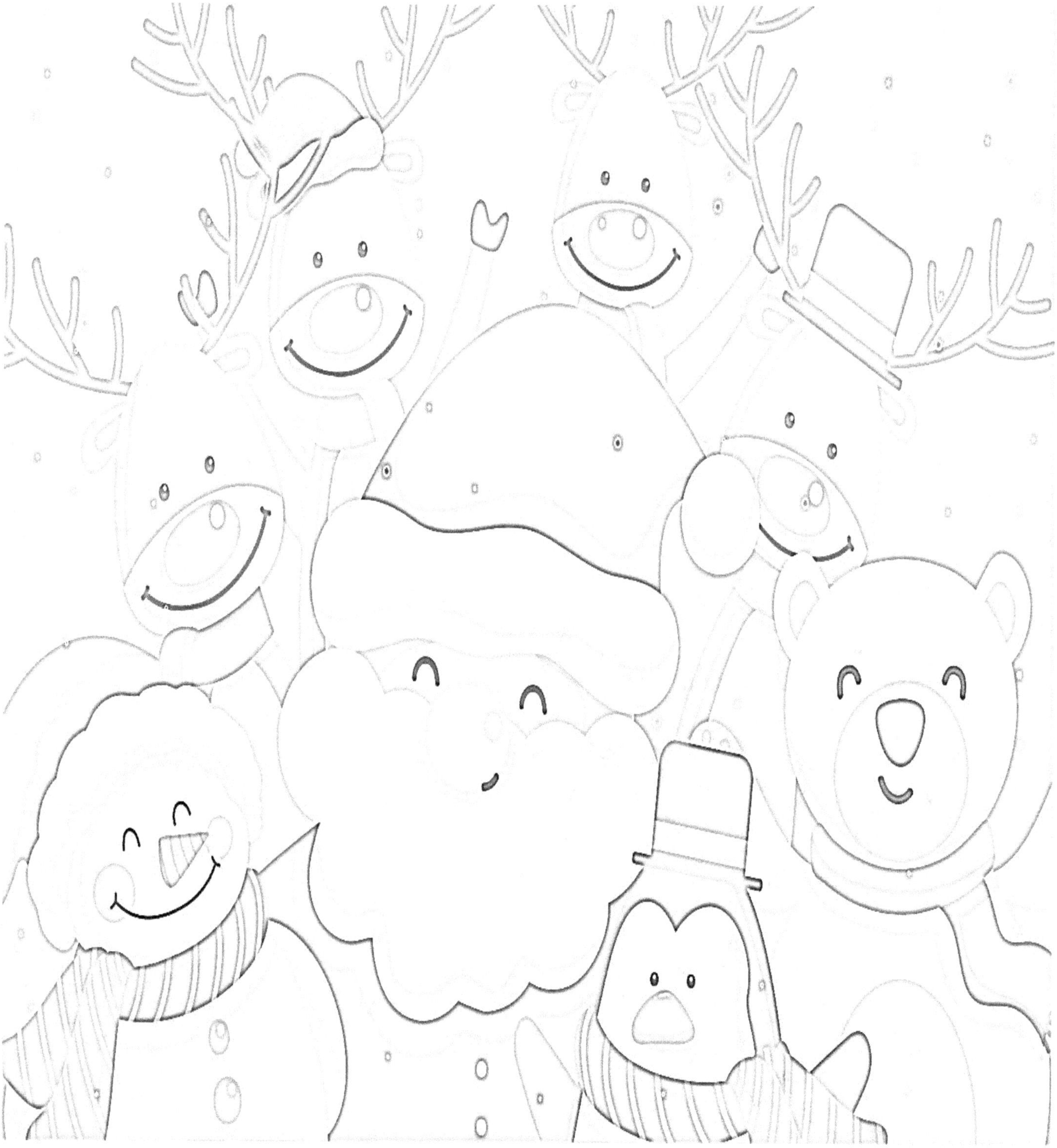

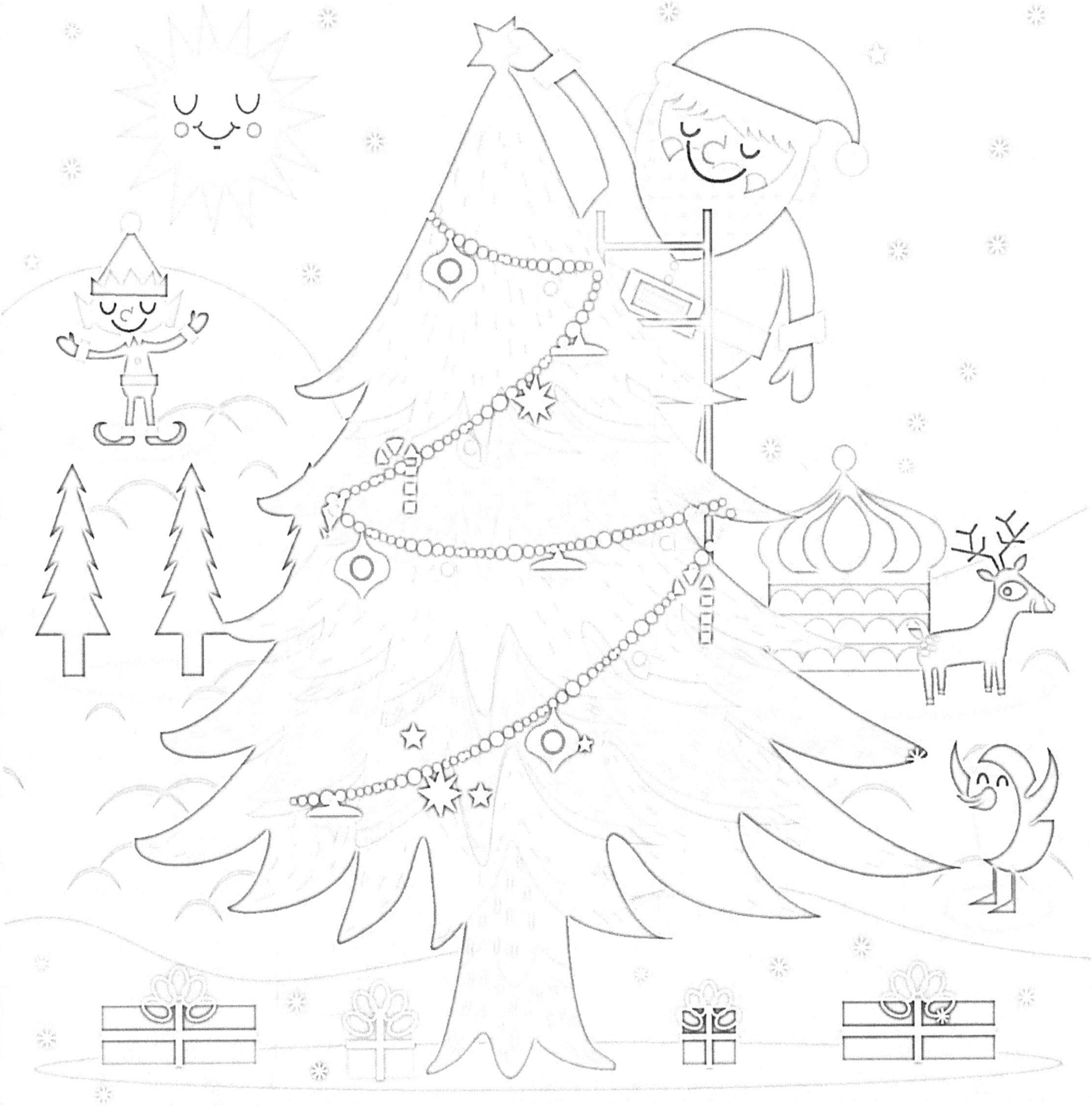

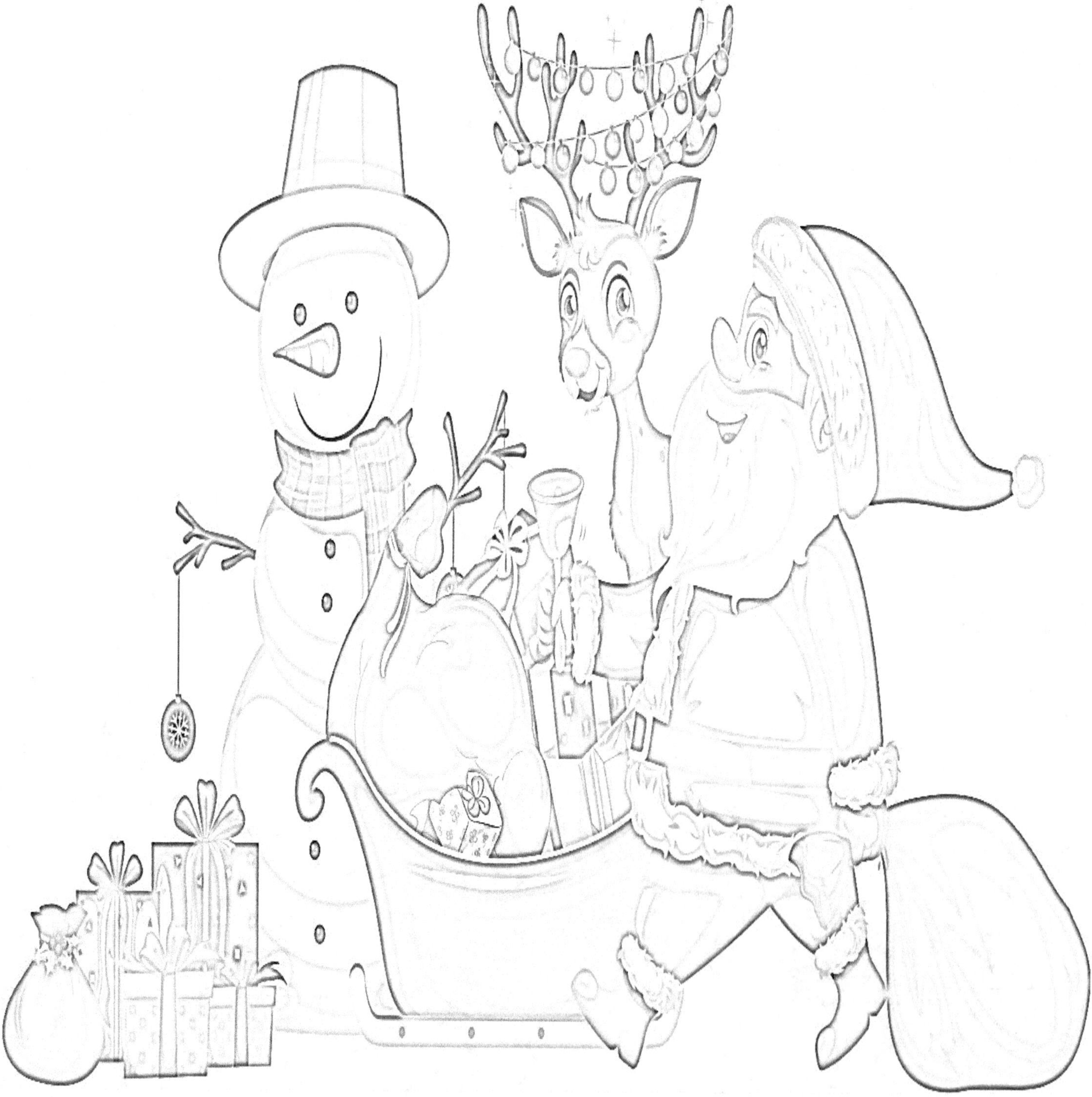

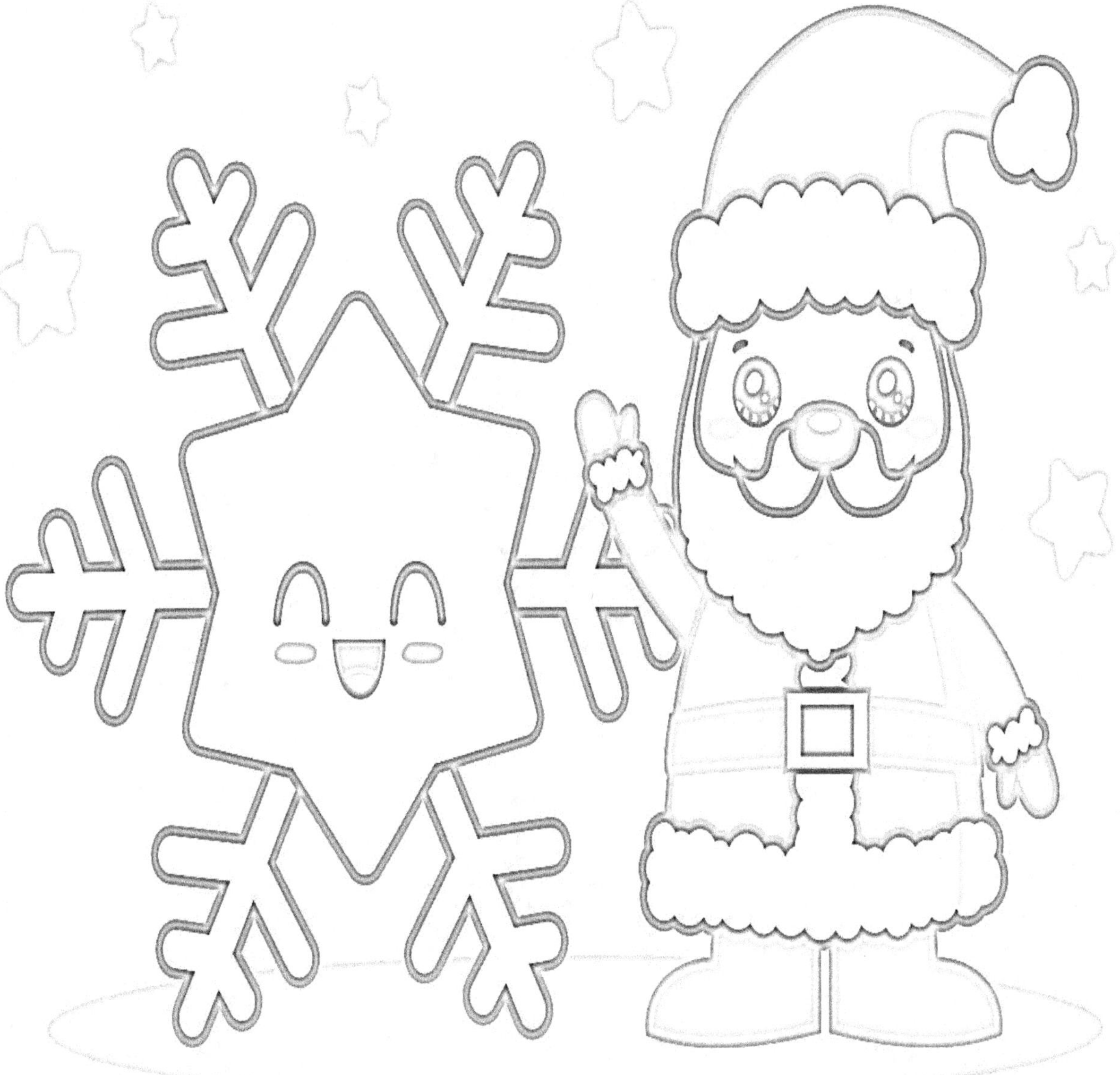

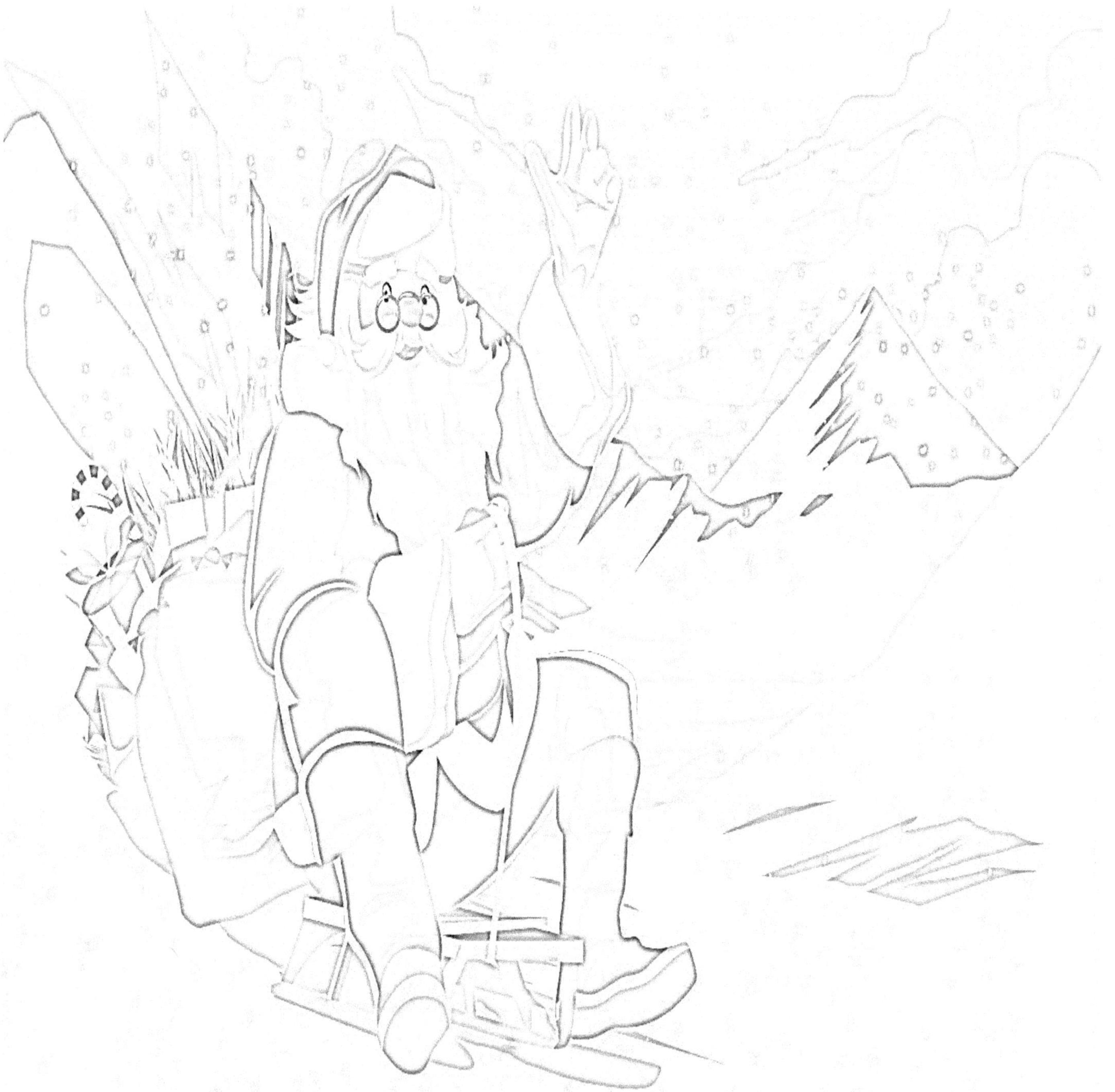

www.ingramcontent.com/pod-product-compliance
Lightning Source LLC
Chambersburg PA
CBHW060437220526
45465CB00008B/3169
* 9 7 9 8 7 5 3 2 4 8 4 1 1 *